The Missing Majority

The Missing Majority

The Recruitment of Women as State Legislative Candidates

David Niven

PRAEGER

Westport, Connecticut
London

Library of Congress Cataloging-in-Publication Data

Niven, David, 1971–
    The missing majority : the recruitment of women as state
legislative candidates / David Niven.
        p.   cm.
    Includes bibliographical references and index.
    ISBN 0–275–96073–0 (alk. paper)
    1. Women political candidates—Recruiting—United States—States.
2. Legislative bodies—United States—States.   3. Sex discrimination
against women—United States.   I. Title.
JK2488.N58   1998
324'.082'0973—dc21   97–26173

British Library Cataloguing in Publication Data is available.

Library of Congress Catalog Card Number: 97–26173
ISBN: 0–275–96073–0

First published in 1998

Praeger Publishers, 88 Post Road West, Westport, CT 06881
An imprint of Greenwood Publishing Group, Inc.

Printed in the United States of America

The paper used in this book complies with the
Permanent Paper Standard issued by the National
Information Standards Organization (Z39.48–1984).

10 9 8 7 6 5 4 3 2 1

*To my mother, Paula Niven, who introduced
me to the phrase, "A woman's place is in the House . . .
and the Senate," before I ever knew there was
anyone who thought differently.*

If liberty and equality,
as is thought by some,
are chiefly to be found in democracy,
they will be best attained when all persons alike
share in the government to the utmost.

—Aristotle

Contents

Tables and Figures

FIGURES

Acknowledgments

I appreciate the efforts of many people whose contributions were essential to this effort. Without the hundreds of county party chairs and women candidates who took the time to complete the survey I sent them, this study would not exist. I also thank the state Democratic and Republican parties of Ohio, New Jersey, California, and Tennessee for providing the addresses of their county chairs, and the National League of Cities for providing the addresses of the women candidates.

This research and these surveys were supported by the Ohio State University Graduate School Alumni Research Award, whose financial help enhanced the breadth of my efforts.

Both the design and presentation of this study have benefited considerably from the input of Lawrence Baum, Paul Allen Beck, and Thomas Nelson. While theirs is the most immediate contribution, I thank all the teachers who have helped along the way.

Finally, I thank the people of New Jersey and Ohio, whose tax dollars paid for my education at Rutgers and Ohio State.

1

Introduction

The image of male leadership as right and proper, and the concomitant image of women as either inadequate or simply incongruent with political power, has been predominant in American political culture. From one of the most respected pieces of research in all of political science scholarship, Converse's belief systems paper (1964), comes this conclusion regarding women's political aptitude:

Now there is one type of relationship in which there is overwhelming evidence for vigorous opinion-leading where politics is concerned in our society. It is the relationship within the family: The wife is very likely to follow her husband's opinions, however imperfectly she may have absorbed their justifications at a more complex level. (233)

The uncomfortabilty with women who are politically active is the subject of a character's comments in John Steinbeck's *Cannery Row* (1945, 200, 204):

"Well," said the captain, "since my wife went into politics, I'm just running crazy. She got elected to the Assembly for this district and when the Legislature isn't in session, she's off making speeches. And when she's home she's studying all the time and writing bills. . . . My wife is a wonderful woman," he said in a kind of peroration. "Most wonderful woman. Ought to of been a man. If she was I wouldn' of married her." He laughed a long time over that and repeated it three or four times and resolved to remember it so he could tell it to a lot of other people.

From the Pulitzer prizewinning account of the 1960 Presidential race, White's (1961) *The Making of the President 1960*, the essence of the relationship between gender and politics is summed up in one sentence, "The root question of American politics is always: Who's the Man to See?" (1936).

These are vignettes from decades ago; surely our society has evolved to become more accepting of women in politics. While that may be true, one does not need to look very hard to find contemporary examples suggesting that politics remains an uneven playing field for men and women.

For example, consider the details of this 1995 t-shirt controversy. "Some Day a Woman Will Be President," was the slogan printed on t-shirts for sale at a Miami Wal-Mart. The implications of this phrase were so disquieting to one Wal-Mart executive, however, that he ordered the shirts removed from the store. The shirts were the creation of psychologist Ann Ruben, who made them in hopes of boosting the self-esteem of girls. Instead, the removal of the shirts illustrated something very different to Ruben: "Promoting females as leaders is still a very threatening concept in this country."[1]

Consistent with the notion that women's political leadership is threatening to some, recent women candidates for office have reported treatment that encouraged them to forego political ambitions. "I've tried to run for the legislature a number of times," said one woman, a locally elected official in California, "but each time there is someone else (always a man) whose turn it's supposed to be." A woman local elected official from Ohio noted that in her party, "It's not the place of women to lead, make the decisions, to take control," or to run for office, because the men in charge of the party "are not comfortable around professional women."[2]

Thus, while women are in the majority in the United States, men tend to dominate positions of political power. For example, in 1997 men hold 79% of the seats at the state legislative level. Women hold significantly more legislative seats today than they did 25 years ago; however, the increase has been slow and has at times stagnated. In no state do women hold more than 38% of the seats in the legislature, and in some states the percentage of women in the legislature remains in single digits (Alabama is currently worst with just 4% of its seats filled by women). Also daunting, in recent state legislative elections, only one-third of the candidates have been women.

While the paucity of women legislators is obviously a statistically unusual pattern, should it merit our concern as an area of study? If it is important to study, then one must wonder who or what is keeping women from legislative office. For example, what ramifications do these sentiments regarding women's incompatibility with political leadership have on women's candidacy rate? The latter questions comprise the underlying mystery that shapes this investigation. As a starting point, this chapter offers an overview of the approach and assumptions that guide this research.

WHY STUDY THE LACK OF WOMEN LEGISLATORS?

While a concern for the process that produces a limited number of elected women may be inherently interesting to students of the inner workings of politics, the issue is also a substantive concern affecting the strength of our democratic government. Darcy, Welch, and Clark (1994) argue that the number of women elected and running for office is of great significance because any exclusion of women translates into the exclusion of some portion of the most talented individuals. These excluded individuals would presumably offer the electorate more and better choices.

Women candidates can also influence the public's behavior. Women legislators can serve as role models for the next generation of women, showing them their potential to serve in a professional capacity (Burrell 1994a; Zepatos and Kaufman 1995; Schramm 1981; Clark and Clark 1984). Also, there is the question of the legitimacy of a system to the public in which half the population is effectively limited to one-fifth or less of the legislative seats. As Norris and Lovenduski (1993, 407) write of the British system, "A parliament which does not look like Britain, no matter how much it claims to speak on behalf of its constituents, remains fundamentally unrepresentative," so too could that be said of a U.S. system that remains woefully short of proportionate representation of women in legislatures (see also, Sapiro 1981a; Saint-Germain 1989). Toward that end, scholars have noted the increased constituency requests women legislators receive compared with male legislators (Thomas 1994; Richardson and Freeman 1995), suggesting that the presence of women does serve to open the doors to government a little wider for the electorate.

Gender and Legislative Output

In addition to the intuitive appeal of creating a deeper talent pool and extending the legitimacy of the system, women legislators are distinct in tangible ways from their male colleagues. Women legislators, in the words of Mezey (1994, 256), simply "understand the needs of women in society in a way that men cannot." This difference manifests itself in the legislative priorities of women legislators (Mezey 1994; Mandel and Dodson 1992; Saint-Germain 1989).

On issues of specific relevance to women, such as reproductive rights, child care, rape and domestic violence, pay equity, and discrimination/harassment, women legislators tend to pay more attention and do more (Mezey 1994; Mandel and Dodson 1992; Saint-Germain 1989). Women legislators not only perceive "women's" issues to be more important, but they tend to believe the support of women constituents is more important for their electoral future than do male legislators (Reingold 1992). Thus, in addition to any priority differences women bring with them to the legislature, they are likely to maintain such differences in an effort to represent their core constituency. Moreover, many believe the effect of women's participation will increase exponentially as they increase their number in legislatures, allowing them greater influence over legislative outcomes (Mezey 1994).

Saint-Germain's (1989) long-term study of legislative action in Arizona provides a good example of the evidence available to establish the difference women legislators make. Studying the initiation and enactment of policy in the Arizona state legislature from 1969 to 1986, Saint-Germain finds that women legislators were more likely to introduce "women's issue" legislation than men. In addition to proposing more legislation in areas of interest to women, women legislators were also more likely to obtain passage for more of their legislation in these areas than men.

Others, such as Berkman and O'Connor (1993), note the important role of women legislators in blocking legislation. Because they are in a seemingly perpetual minority, women legislators are often a more powerful coalition in blocking legislation, especially in committees where women may predominate, than they are in passing legislation, which ultimately requires a majority of the body.

This is especially true because women are disproportionately likely to serve on certain committees, such as those dealing with education or health and human services. Berkman and O'Connor find this potential power manifests itself in the abortion issue, where states with large numbers of women on the health and human services committees are less likely to have passed legislation limiting abortion access.

The differences between men and women legislators go beyond the way they vote on legislation, however. Some argue that their fundamental approach to governing differs. Kathlene (1989, 1995) argues that men and women conceptualize issues, problems, and government solutions quite differently.

In a study conducted in 1985, Kathlene (1989) read Colorado state legislators a newspaper article on underweight infants. The article detailed a study done by county health workers that found alarming numbers of underweight infants, especially in poor homes. The article noted that the county involved wanted to increase efforts to educate younger parents about the nutritional needs of infants.

The male legislators' reaction to the article was strikingly different than the reaction of the female legislators. For example, Kathlene quotes one male legislator:

Well, my first reaction, I don't necessarily think it's a problem. I think we worry a little too much about people, it may be a problem but I don't know if it is something that needs anything done about it. I mean, it's talking about underweight babies, babies that are below normal. I mean I don't know, if I read that article, just read that in the paper, I'd say "isn't that interesting" and turn the page. You know, not worry about this thing. (1989, 410)

Conversely, female legislators typically said that this was a serious situation that demanded a government response. The women were much more likely, in fact, to address the problem itself, while the men were more fixated on whether this was a problem and then debated its proper categorization. While none of the women questioned whether this was a subject that public officials should be involved in, many men seemed reluctant to "interfere" in the lives of the families involved. In other words, most male legislators questioned whether this was a problem at all, and to the extent it was a problem, many men thought it a private problem, therefore a non-problem in public policy terms. This philosophy was articulated by many male legislators, including one who argued:

But I don't know what kind of project that you go with on something like that because you're intruding. And maybe these families want to have their children thin. Maybe that's the way that they feel like its a healthier thing. Do we impose saying, putting on a scale when you are five years old you're supposed to weigh 69 pounds, or you don't do that. I think it's up to the family, an individual right. (1989, 413)

In a study conducted in 1989 with similar methods, Kathlene (1995) had Colorado state legislators read an article on recidivism rates, and then solicited their thoughts. She found that women were more likely to see the problem as complex and multi-faceted, where men were more apt to see simple solutions. To wit, women were concerned with the origins of crime, the likely effects of societal problems on a person, and the importance of education and economic opportunity in influencing behavior. Men were more likely to attribute criminal behavior to individuals' character flaws, as one male legislator said of criminals, "They've made that as a choice, of a life-style, and just keeping them off the street doesn't change that mind set" (1995, 708).

These differences in approach had quite meaningful public policy implications. To reduce crime, men reacted by trying to make prison more of a punishment, to "quit treating them like hotel guests," as one male legislator put it (1995, 710). Women's reactions typically emphasized the need to make the prisons more useful conduits of rehabilitation. In fact, Kathlene finds that the legislative proposals of the men and women legislators conformed to this tendency, with the different approaches eventually resulting in men and women introducing quite different pieces of legislation to combat crime.

Gender and Legislative Conduct

In addition to votes and approaches to issues, men and women are found to "legislate" differently. That is to say, while their goals are different, their behavior in pursuit of their goals can also be quite distinct.

Rosenthal (1996), using a 1994 mail survey of state legislative committee chairs in all 50 states, asked legislators directly about their tendency to see their task as one of collective enterprise versus one of personal power. Rosenthal found that women chairs were much more likely to emphasize the importance of getting members involved, in building coalitions, and in making the process work for all concerned. These women leaders were much more likely to stress discussion and more likely to stress fairness, and to acknowledge the collaborative process of legislating. In short, Rosenthal concludes, women want to win by convincing others of the merits of their position. Men, on the other hand, value winning by dominating, by using their power to see that their position is ultimately victorious, rather than concerning themselves with the opinions of the minority (see also Kathlene 1994).

Ultimately, whether one focuses on legislative output, legislative style, legitimacy, or the mere size of the available talent pool, scholars in women and politics research argue persuasively that the processes that influence the number of women elected are of significance to anyone affected by the output, existence, or make-up of legislatures.

The State Legislative Level

Study of women on the state legislative level, specifically, is of interest for a number of reasons. First, given the evolving priorities of the federal government, state governments have expanded their responsibilities in providing services and have generally taken a more activist role (Van Horn 1993). Second, the state legislature is a very important stepping stone for higher office. State legislatures are breeding grounds for future members of Congress as well as for state-level offices (Fowler and McClure 1989). Thus, to be excluded from state legislative service is to be excluded from a rapidly expanding level of government and to face a reduced chance of a rapidly expanding electoral career.

BARRIERS KEEPING WOMEN FROM LEGISLATIVE OFFICE

If study of the dearth of women state legislators is warranted, what are the potential causes of this pattern? First, consider that in a traditional conception of the electoral process (depicted in Figure 1.1) there are four main actors involved in officeholder selection: candidates, voters, contributors, and elites (Werner 1993; Leowenberg and Patterson 1979). Potentially, any or all of these actors may be inhibiting women from running for or gaining elective office.

The candidate explanation holds that women may be less likely to secure legislative office because of their own traits or dispositions. Research in this area has focused on differences between men and women with regard to resources, interest, and ambition. At various times all three of these variables were thought to be adequate explanations for the lack of women officeholders because each was thought to explain why women were not coming forward as candidates. Over time, however, the disparity in resources (such as education and income), interest in politics, and ambition for office have either been decreasing or discredited as sufficient explanatory factors.

If it is not something inherent in women that is deterring them from offering themselves as candidates, perhaps it is a lack of support from voters or financial contributors that dooms women who do decide to run for office. Numerous studies, however, examining both election returns and experimental data, have concluded that women are not significantly deterred from gaining office by voters (see, for example, Burrell 1994a). Similar results regarding campaign contributions have been reached after examining the financial statements of male and female candidates for state legislative seats and Congress (see, for example, Darcy, Welch, and Clark 1994).

The conclusion that neither lack of ability or interest on the part of women, nor discrimination at the hands of voters or contributors, are adequate explanations for the dearth of women legislators naturally led to scrutiny of the fourth actor in the process, elites. Specifically, the attitudes of political party elites could play an important and somewhat hidden role in the process of electing legislators. Despite the importance of party elites, with their ability to encourage potential candidates, discourage potential candidates, groom people for political activity, and influence

Figure 1.1
Model of the Electoral Process

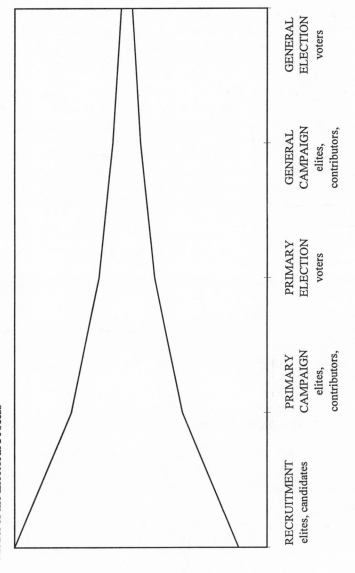

RECRUITMENT
elites, candidates

PRIMARY
CAMPAIGN
elites,
contributors,

PRIMARY
ELECTION
voters

GENERAL
CAMPAIGN
elites,
contributors,

GENERAL
ELECTION
voters

Source: Adapted from Werner 1993; Leowenberg and Patterson 1979.

candidate success, the role and importance of elites is perhaps the least understood of the four groups of actors considered here.

Studies indicate that political party elites influence who runs for the legislature, and therefore influence who wins legislative seats (Frendreis, Gibson, and Vertz 1990). As a consequence of their influence over the process, elites are clearly in a position to affect the number of women who seek legislative office.

Despite the importance of the relationship between party recruiters and potential women candidates, little has been done to directly study this interaction. While the gravamen of past research suggests that elites are not biased against women, much of the work on recruiters is limited by the data utilized. For example, much of the work has relied on reports of treatment received by successful candidates (see, for example, McLean 1994). Successful candidates are an obviously unrepresentative group in comparison with the universe of potential candidates, many of whom were presumably discouraged from running. Such a sample, in fact, excludes people who were most likely to suffer bias, thus greatly compromising the veracity of resulting conclusions absolving elites of any bias against women candidates. Even the most comprehensive assessments of party recruiter behavior have been made by inferring their attitudes from political outcomes rather than by examining party recruiters directly (see Werner 1993).

The significance of elites is magnified by their position in the electoral process. Elites stand with candidates at the first gate of the electoral obstacle course (see Figure 1.1). In other words, their influence is felt when the widest array of people are available to move forward. Further, their initial decisions are made when there are likely many objectively similar potential candidates who must begin to be whittled down to the candidate of choice.

Despite their obvious interest in finding the most capable candidates, there is reason to suspect recruiters might not be above bias. Some would argue that their position of authority feeds a rigidity of beliefs (see, for example, Jackman and Muha 1984). This rigidity encourages recruiters to make decisions without questioning their own motives or thought processes. Further, the process of expectancy effects, where the recruiters' expectations might influence the behavior of the prospective candidate, can serve to offer an illusory confirmation of the recruiters' beliefs.

Unfortunately, the conclusions of work on elite bias in recruiting are both rudimentary and conflicting. As a result, there is disagreement over how much bias against women exists among party elites, and even less is known about what might create such bias.

Previous research thus leads us to this point. The lack of women state legislators does not seem to be fully accounted for by qualities of the women, nor of the voters, nor of contributors. While the thrust of research on elites would cast doubt on allegations of their being biased, the quality of information available on elites is much weaker. Therefore, the potential for expanding our understanding of why there are few women legislators seems most likely to be in examination of elite recruiter behavior.

WHITHER STUDIES OF ELITES?

Given its promise, why has the interaction between the recruitment process and the decisions of potential female candidates not been adequately studied? One reason has to do with the difficulty of the undertaking. Darcy, Welch, and Clark (1994), authors of a comprehensive treatment of women and elections, notably assert that:

trying to figure out who constitutes a pool of potential candidates and then learning the members' reasons for running or not are nearly impossible tasks. So our conclusions about why women do not run must be based more on inference and less on direct evidence than our conclusions about what happens to women when they do run. (178)

To argue that it is "nearly impossible" to study potential candidates is, however, an overstatement. Studies of recruiters and potential candidates do exist (see Fowler and McClure 1989; Canon, Schousen, and Sellers 1994; Abel and Oppenheimer 1994; Herrnson and Tennant 1994; Hertzke 1994; Kazee and Roberts 1994; Haskell, Sutten, and Squire 1994; Copeland 1994; Layzell and Overby 1994). However, these studies do not probe for the causes or roots of the treatment women receive in the recruitment process.

Unfortunately, most studies on recruitment and candidacies of women focus only on actual candidates (see, for example, Carroll 1994; Darcy, Welch, and Clark 1994). This is a problem for this area of study, as Baer (1993) argues that our picture of women's recruitment is largely drawn from women candidates, a very narrow group that misses both the recruiters and those who decided against running. This is akin to trying to understand a championship team's success without mentioning the coaches or the opposing teams.

Baer further argues that the domination of the survey research approach, focusing on voters' reactions to candidates, has limited our knowledge of the process by which women come to be under-represented. She alludes to the old piece of wisdom, "Give a small boy a hammer, and he finds everything he encounters needs pounding," in arguing that survey research capabilities have been over-utilized by scholars interested in women and politics merely because they were available and not because they were informative (Baer 1993, 550). Instead, Baer (1993) and Burrell (1986) both argue that more attention should be paid to parties and their recruitment of potential candidates. Parties have different cultures and mechanisms with regard to women and women candidates, yet little has been done to establish the consequences of the parties' actions (Freeman 1986). Method and focus matter when examining women and politics material because they can change the answers one finds. If one asks questions in a survey that touch upon possible discrimination and directs the questions at a limited field of actors, one will likely find a very different answer than if all the relevant actors are studied with a device sensitive to socially desirable responses.

Two interesting examples of the importance of method in studies of women and politics demonstrate the different answers produced by different methods. Werner

(1993) shows that aggregate data can frequently mask differential treatment of women. Bias may be hidden in aggregation when variation between and within states is ignored. Werner's results would have shown no bias against women at the state level, but a breakdown within states revealed that certain areas were less favorable for women's candidacies. Most studies of women's political fortunes have aggregated as much as possible in the name of comprehensiveness. Darcy, Welch, and Clark (1994), for example, examine data comparing how women and men candidates fare in the aggregate for a number of states at a number of points in time. Such a procedure may have obscured bias evident in smaller units.

Another example of the method changing the answer exists in Blair and Henry's (1981) examination of the family factor in candidates' decisions. Blair and Henry find that the family is often overlooked in reports of men's decisions to run, but emphasized in studies of women. The greater family emphasis for women had been assumed to reflect reality. However, Blair and Henry caution that another reason two different levels of emphasis on family emerge is that two different methods are used. Studies of women have tended to include surveys and interviews of women candidates and have asked specifically about family. Studies of male legislators, on the other hand, have tended to be aggregate data analyses in which the focus has been on easily available data, such as legislative salary. When Blair and Henry apply the survey and interview method to male candidates, they find that the responses are much more family oriented, not unlike the traditional wisdom on women.

It is obviously important to apply appropriate methods to the study of the recruitment of women candidates and to study all parties involved. Thus, while there are a number of studies that argue women are not subject to bias, all too often these studies offer stronger conclusions than evidence.

A STUDY OF THE PARTY ELITE/CANDIDATE INTERACTION

Given its promise and the importance of attempting anew to apply appropriate methods, it is the party elites' attitudes, behavior, and their ramifications on potential women candidates that this research will explore. Two vital questions arise when examining the relationship between elites and potential women candidates: How much elite bias exists? and What motivates biased behavior?

Psychological scholarship informs the effort to explain bias, as psychologists have dedicated great efforts toward the end of understanding the processes and habits that lead to irrational decision making, of which bias against members of a group is one important example (for review, see Fiske and Taylor 1991, chapters 6-9). Based on a review of the applicable literature, it is hypothesized that bias against women candidates is most likely based on one of two perceptual processes: the outgroup effect or the distribution effect.

In brief, the outgroup effect involves the tendency to relate positively to those we see as being similar to ourselves, while those we see as dissimilar are thought to be part of a homogenous and less valued group. The outgroup effect is a compelling explanation of bias in the recruitment of women because most party leaders are male. For male party leaders, assumptions regarding females translate into assumptions involving an outgroup. Members of the outgroup are frequently lumped together in a person's mind, such that negative qualities associated with the group are associated with all the individual members of that group (Judd and Park 1988). If male party leaders hold the view that people similar to themselves are more politically capable, one would expect that prospective female candidates would be lumped into an outgroup in which the default assumption is that a woman is not as politically capable as a man. In essence, according to the logic of the outgroup effect, lack of similarity between female candidates and the predominantly male party elite makes the party elite less likely to recognize or assume the merits of a potential female candidate.

A competing explanation for biased treatment of women by party leaders is the distribution effect. Here the differential distribution of men and women into distinct productive roles feeds the creation of gender-based assessments (Eagly and Wood 1982). Because of sexual segregation in work roles, men outnumber women in positions of achievement, and women more frequently have low-status jobs. This results in abstractions of the sexes based on their distribution in productive roles (Yount 1986). Thus, because women are more likely to pursue home-based or low-status work than are men, and because women officeholders are comparatively rare, party leaders encountering a woman interested in political office could subconsciously assume that men are more likely to succeed in politics given their relative distribution.

Thus, the key distinction between the two effects is whether similarity with the evaluator (outgroup effect) or similarity with those in positions of achievement (distribution effect) fosters positive evaluation. Table 1.1 presents a brief encapsulation of the two effects. Further details and examples of the outgroup and distribution effects are provided in Chapter 3.

At its most basic level, this research will explore the attitudes of elites and potential women candidates as part of an effort to determine the prevalence, origins, and ramifications of each form of bias in the recruitment process. In other words, this effort will work toward the end of understanding how well the interaction between party recruiters and potential women candidates accounts for the lack of women legislators while attempting to understand how bias affects that interaction.

At its root, recruitment is studied because the process of selecting our leaders profoundly affects how vague community interests are translated into public policy. This research will most directly have relevance to the mystery of why few women are in a position to enact their vision of the community's interest. This study will also be relevant to the broader field of recruitment, illuminating whether similarity to the evaluator or similarity to the previously successful are necessary attributes for any potential candidates to be warmly received--in other words, helping us to better understand how all the arbiters of community interest achieve that status.

Table 1.1
Encapsulation of Outgroup and Distribution Effects

OUTGROUP EFFECT

origin:	subject's lack of similarity with evaluator
result:	feeds doubts (lack of positive association fostered by similarity), tendency to homogenize, tendency to exaggerate traits
for women candidates:	where party chair is male, harder to gain acceptance

DISTRIBUTION EFFECT

origin:	subject's lack of similarity with those in position of achievement (e.g., elected politicians)
result:	feeds doubts about appropriateness of subject, preference for those who resemble successful, more confidence in those who resemble successful
for women candidates:	where women are not prevalent in politics, harder to gain acceptance

In addition to developing a picture of the landscape in which potential women candidates exist today, this research has implications for the future. The prevalence of the two hypothesized forms of party recruiter bias, the distribution and outgroup effects, needs to be studied further because the future ramifications of the two processes differ greatly. More optimistically, the distribution effect suggests that as the number of women in high-status positions increases, elites will react by increasing their acceptance and enthusiasm for female candidacies because their perception of the distribution of roles will change. The outgroup effect, more ominously, would predict that male party elites will remain reluctant to support female candidacies regardless of the number of women in high-status positions.

More broadly considered, this effort is also quite relevant to scholarly controversies regarding political parties and political psychology. Viewed from the aggregate, or in the abstract, it follows that in an era of candidate-centered, entrepreneurial politics, parties represent a decreasing force in American politics (see, for example, Maisel 1981). Others, often taking a more in-depth, case study-style approach to examine small units of party behavior, assert that parties continue to play an important role in encouraging and discouraging political activity, such as running for office (see, for example, Hertzke 1994). This study offers a more comprehensive approach than the latter while trying to achieve a more detailed analysis than might have been possible in the former. If party elites prove to have significant influence on women's candidacy rate, this will serve to help us not only better understand how women are elected but how relevant political parties and their leaders are in the candidate creation process.

Meanwhile, debate continues over the applicability of psychological tendencies found in the laboratory to real-world political behavior (see, for example, Lau 1995; Fazio and Williams 1986). Psychological studies play an important role in establishing a foundation for the expectations concerning the attitudes explored here. Support or rejection of these expectations will offer useful evidence for scholars wishing to assess the relevance and implications of laboratory psychological scholarship for elite political behavior.

Finally, this research will improve on previous work in the field in a number of significant areas. First, to gain a better understanding of a process in which two very different actors fundamentally affect the outcome, both elites and potential candidates will be examined. Second, instead of inferring their motives or attitudes from loosely related behavior, the assessment of both elites and potential candidates will rely on more direct measures of attitudes. Third, this examination begins with a theoretical foundation on perceptual biases that hopefully lends both purpose and clarity to this attempt to better understand the recruitment of prospective women legislative candidates.

PRESENTATION OF RESULTS

Chapter 2 will present a review of previous evidence, highlighting the promise of studying the role of party elites and their interaction with potential candidates.

Chapter 3 offers an overview of the two hypothesized forms of perceptual bias and the research design with which the existence, origins, and ramifications of bias will be studied. Chapter 4 begins the presentation of data as the prevalence of the outgroup and distribution effects are examined with an aggregate level approach. Chapter 5 explores the correlates or determinants of bias. Chapter 6 offers estimates of the ramifications of bias on women's candidacies. Chapter 7 presents conclusions and implications of the findings.

NOTES

1. Trisha Flynn, "Corporation Quakes, All Because of a T-Shirt Message," *Rocky Mountain News*, October 15, 1995, p. 72A.

2. Comments are from author's survey of women elected on the local level (details of survey provided in Chapter 3).

2

Research on Women's Candidacy Rate: The Promise of Studying Elites

Previous scholarly work on the question of why few women hold state legislative office can be broken into two major groups. The first area explored was supply-based explanations, which focused on the lack of interested and capable women. More recently, attention has shifted to demand-based explanations, which focus on possible bias against women from sources including voters, contributors, or party elites. This chapter reviews previous explanations for the lack of women legislators and explores the promise of studying the role of elites in the candidacy process.

Vast scholarly evidence on legislative elections and candidate behavior casts doubt on the sufficiency of explanations blaming women for a lack of ability or interest. After the adequacy of supply-based explanations was questioned by scholars, demand for women candidates was studied, first with an eye toward voter bias. Research, however, failed to support the notion that voter or contributor prejudice significantly reduced the demand for female candidates.

Party elites were naturally the next subject of investigation. This was the case not merely because the other explanations had failed to fully account for the lack of women legislators, but also because party leaders play an important role in determining who runs for office and, by extension, who wins office. When party elites advise, encourage, and discourage women, they are influencing the decisions of potential women candidates. In the process, party elites are not only affecting how many women candidates proceed but also what types of women candidates proceed. While it seems quite important and promising, the study of the recruiter/candidate interaction has nevertheless been limited and remains in need of a more comprehensive treatment.

SUPPLY OF CANDIDATES

Resources

Understanding how the recruitment of women candidates has emerged as a most promising focus for explaining the lack of women officeholders requires exploring the most important alternate accounts concerning why few women hold office. For many years, supply-based explanations were emphasized by women and politics scholars. The supply of female candidates first depends upon the number of women who have the skills and resources to seek and hold office. As Dubeck (1976) points out, the critical resources that lead to success in the private sector (such as education) are the same factors that foster political success. There is, in a sense, an "eligible pool" of potential officeholders--people who come from the highest strata of education and income and who could feasiblely mount a political campaign (Gertzog 1979; Welch 1978; Darcy, Welch, and Clark 1994). While women in the aggregate suffer from holding fewer resources, which limits their political activity, Schlozman, Burns, and Verba (1994) find that equalizing resources would serve to equalize political activity for men and women. Thus, one would expect that members of the eligible pool, who by definition have similar resources, would engage in politics at similar levels regardless of gender. At the same time, to the extent that there are fewer women in the eligible pool, one would expect there to be fewer female officeholders.

Evidence supporting the eligible pool explanation from congressional races and state legislative races has shown that successful female candidates tend to have much the same demographic background as successful male candidates (Carroll 1994; Diamond 1977; Bullock and Heys 1972; Nechemias 1987), and that as the level of education for women rises in a state or district, the number of elected women rises (Jones and Nelson 1981; Nechemias 1987; Rule 1987; Green 1995). The power of the eligible pool explanation breaks down, though, because estimates show that there are between two and three times as many women in the eligible pool as one would expect to find given the number of women in elected office (Welch 1978; Rule 1981). Further, variation in the size of the eligible pool in each state is a very weak predictor of female representation in state legislatures (Welch 1978).

Interest

Another possible cause of the low supply of female legislators could be lack of interest in politics on the part of eligible women. Obviously, the number of women in the eligible pool will not account for female representation if those women are less likely to be interested in politics than eligible men. Early studies argued that, in fact, women were less interested in politics; the dynamics of socialization, school training, and family life created a situation where the female had no inclination to pursue politics (Lane 1959; Hyman 1959). Lane emphasized that the dependent and receptive role of women was unsuited to political activity, as men were generally expected to make all important decisions.

The lack of interest hypothesis suffers, however, when several national studies of politically active people are examined. These studies indicate that while there is certainly a lack of female officeholders, there are tremendous numbers of women participating in the political process by working or volunteering for political parties and campaigns (Sapiro and Farah 1980; Costantini and Craik 1972; Clark, Hadley, and Darcy 1989). If women are active in party politics and political campaigns, then it is obviously not an inherent lack of interest in politics that is holding women back.

More recent work has argued that while women may not be socialized away from politics, they may be socialized away from playing certain roles in politics. A number of scholars have argued that men are more likely to adopt an external focus, attempting to play a role in wide-ranging processes. Women, on the other hand, tend toward an internal focus where they attempt to work on tasks that concern their immediate group (Costantini and Craik 1972; Sapiro 1982). It has also been argued that women tend to avoid taking a position of visible dominance (Sapiro and Farah 1980), which is suggested by evidence that women are less likely to try to influence another person's vote (Welch 1977). Women have also been shown to be less focused on self-advancement, both in terms of expanding their political position and in matters such as expanding their business contacts through politics (Fowlkes, Perkins, and Rinehart 1979; Costantini and Bell 1984).

Given these arguments, it is not very surprising to find that women and men who are interested and active in the same political party wind up performing very different tasks. Women are more likely to work on the party infrastructure, while men are more likely to work to widen the party's appeal in many ways, including running for office (Fowlkes, Perkins, and Rinehart 1979; Margolis 1980). Indeed, studies of delegates to state and national party conventions indicate that women delegates have less ambition to run for office than men delegates (Sapiro and Farah 1980; Jennings and Thomas 1968; Jennings and Farah 1981; Clark, Hadley, and Darcy 1989; Costantini 1990; but see Carroll 1985).

With all the findings showing men to be more ambitious than women, scholars wondered about the factors that created this ambition gap, as well as those factors that influenced the politically ambitious women who did exist. Many expected to find dramatic effects of socialization. For example, politically active women might have had a unique pattern of socialization, involving perhaps a politically active mother. This was found to be true; however, it was true for both politically active women and men. The ambitious were far more distinct from non-ambitious political people than the male ambitious were distinct from the female (Diamond 1977; Merritt 1980; Jennings and Thomas 1968; Clark, Hadley, and Darcy 1989; Fowlkes 1984b). In other words, both politically ambitious men and women were apparently countersocialized away from the norm of little activity.

One thing that many of these studies have in common is that the documented differences between men and women are shrinking for almost all political measures (Soule and McGrath 1977). Toward that end, work on people who were raised in the 1960s and later shows much less difference between males and females with regard to political opinions and interest (Orum, Cohen, Grasmuck, and Orum 1977; Thornton, Alwin, and Camburn 1983). Another important finding is that the ambition gap is larger as the office in question is more prestigious (Jennings and Farah 1981). The ambition gap for the U.S. Senate is huge, but the gap for the state legislature is essentially non-existent. These two findings suggest relevant differences between men and women are shrinking and are not particularly significant on the state legislative level.

While childhood socialization is often the target of blame for the lack of women officeholders, effects of childhood are mitigated by adult experiences, which are frequently credited for encouraging the women who do pursue politics. Mezey (1980), in fact, argues that childhood socialization is not important when compared to the role of adult experiences in determining political activity. Education and working are seen as providing women with the resources, interest, and personality development that facilitate participation in politics (Jacob 1962; Andersen and Cook 1985; Clark, Hadley, and Darcy 1989; Rossi 1983; Costantini 1990; Fowlkes 1984b). To wit, survey work has shown that once women attain a college education, the differences in socialization for men and women have very little influence on political interest (Tedin, Brady, and Vedlitz 1977).

Another adult experience, being involved in some form of voluntary organization, can also increase political activity (Rosenstone and Hansen 1993). Organizations, both political and non-political, serve as a training ground for organizing skills and as a source of professional contacts that may increase the relevance of political events (Rossi 1983). Organizations not only provide women with an activity in which they suffer no access bias based on gender, but also have the side effect of affecting more strongly women's interest and activity in politics than men's (Schlozman, Burns, and Verba 1994). Moreover, there are groups specifically concerned with women's rights which tend to make salient the need for women to band together to fight for specific causes while simultaneously providing an infrastructure to make that effort possible (Mandel 1981; Volgy, Schwarz, and Gottlieb 1986; Clark, Hadley, and Darcy 1989). Some groups go as far as announcing political openings, grooming candidates, and raising money for them (Flammang 1984). The importance of groups in the women election equation is emphasized by Volgy, Schwarz, and Gottlieb (1986) because, unlike other socializing forces, groups are dynamic. Childhood experiences and even career patterns do not tend to change dramatically in six months, but a new organization could do just that, helping to explain the vicissitudes of elections.

In addition to these positive forces limiting the weight of the socialization argument, if women were simply seeking to avoid confrontation or lacked political ambition (as the socialization argument suggests), then we would not expect to see the candidacy rate of women jump when their children reach young adulthood. Thus, another explanation centers on the family role of women. Women are frequently expected to maintain primary responsibility for their children, even when both parents work. The need to care for a family could obviously depress women's inclination to run for office.

Studies of females interested in politics have found that the potential irregularity and long hours of political officeholding make many mothers very hesitant to consider such a move (Lee 1976, 1977; Diamond 1977; Carroll 1994; Mezey 1978a, 1980; Sapiro 1982; Currey 1977; Merritt 1980). In addition to the concerns voiced by women legislators and prospective women legislators, Nechemias (1985) argues that the family constraint on women's political careers is evident in the geographical distribution of women legislators. Nechemias finds that women legislators live closer to the state capital, on average, than do their male colleagues. This suggests to Nechemias that women forego legislative careers when the travel would require them to spend too much time away from home. Studlar and McAllister (1991) extend the argument by noting that for men a family is a fundamental political asset that can be displayed on the campaign trail, while for women a family can foreclose any chance of political office.

Fortunately for the politically interested female, children grow up and become less of a burden on time and resources. Thus, as women become older they are more likely to pursue political office (Sapiro and Farah 1980). However, research on political ambition emphasizes the rational progression of ambition as a person's situation evolves (Black 1972). As a person ages, the list of offices she or he can realistically aspire to shrinks because of the time needed to establish oneself in lower office and to wait for the appropriate chance to contest for higher office (Hain 1974). Many argue this is of great significance for women since women's family commitments encourage them to start their political careers somewhat later in life (Smith 1976; Merritt 1980; Briscoe 1989).

Despite the historical significance and intuitive appeal, the family factor explanation has two major limitations that prevent it from explaining the dearth of women in state legislatures. First, even if women delayed their entry into politics because of child-raising responsibilities, this pattern at best would help to explain why there are few women at the uppermost reaches of political office, since there is a time constraint on women's efforts for political advancement. This, however, does not explain why there are so few women in state houses, which are offices typically requiring far less experience. Moreover, McLean (1994) argues that the delay in women's entry has shrunken to the point where it generally does not significantly curb their ambition. The second limitation is that scholars who have dedicated the same resources to examining the decisions of men in legislative elections have found family considerations to be a major influence on them as well (Norris and Lovenduski 1993; Blair and Henry 1981; Hertzke 1994).

Other than age, women's announced ambition appears to be limited by a greater sense of reality (Bledsoe and Herring 1990; Burt-Way and Kelly 1991). Bledsoe and Herring find that female city council members have more accurate perceptions of their chances of re-election and their chances for advancement than do male council members. This sense of reality should not be dismissed as the pessimism of a beaten-down class, as it exists among women who have already won office and appear to have reasonably calculated that their influence and prospects for continued election are highest at the local and state legislative level (Carroll 1994; Burt-Way and Kelly 1991).

Notably, neither Bledsoe and Herring nor scholars offering some of the strongest conclusions regarding socialization, ambition, and the family factor find evidence that these influences are important on the state legislative level. Offices above the state legislative level may be subject to a lack of interested women since age and realism may limit women's initiative. Conversely, the state legislature is a low enough office that, despite a generally lower level of announced ambition across the spectrum of political offices, women aspire to it at essentially equal levels as men (Jennings and Farah 1981; McLean 1994).[1]

While the supply of female candidates may not be quite as large as the supply of male candidates for the state legislature, there is reason to believe that there are disproportionately more capable and interested women than there are candidates (Welch 1978; Carroll 1994). Based on her survey results, McLean (1994) concludes that the assertion that women lack the ambition or resources necessary to win office is unsubstantiated. Tremendous energy has been expended exploring the supply explanation for the lack of women officeholders, but ultimately the great thrust of evidence is that, as McLean (1994) alluded, women officeholders are not primarily in short supply due to any deficiency among women. If the supply of women is an insufficient answer, attention must focus on demand for women candidates. In short, the demand for women candidates would be limited if either the voters, contributors, or elites (who participate in the recruitment of candidates) construct barriers for the prospective female officeholder.

DEMAND FOR CANDIDATES

Voters

The first arbiters of demand are the voters. If voters in the United States are uncomfortable with female candidates, it would obviously be very hard to elect female representatives. Despite this potential area of concern, many studies have asserted that when one controls for incumbency and party, there is no discernable voter bias against women legislative candidates (U.S. studies: Burrell 1988, 1990, 1992, 1994a; Bernstein 1986; Bullock and Johnson 1985; Herrick 1995; Karnig and Walter 1976; Zipp and Plutzer 1985; Darcy and Schramm 1977; Darcy, Brewer, and Clay 1984; Darcy, Welch, and Clark 1994; Ambrosius and Welch 1984; Bledsoe and Herring 1990; Carroll 1994; Clark, Darcy, Welch, and Ambrosius 1984; McLean 1994; Hausman 1994; Gaddie and Bullock 1995; Paolino 1995; other democracies: Studlar and McAllister 1991; Studlar and Welch 1987; Welch and Studlar 1988, 1990; Rasmussen 1983). Experimental and survey designs have also shown the public to be supportive of hypothetical female candidates (Sigelman and Welch 1984; Welch and Sigelman 1982; Ekstrand and

Eckert 1981; Huddy and Terkildsen 1993b; Rosenwasser et al. 1987; Kaid, Myers, Pipps, and Hunter 1984; Burrell 1994a; Hedlund, Freeman, Hamm, and Stein 1979). Based on the sum of scholarly work, one would conclude that women leaders do not appear to be threatening to the electorate, as women candidates are not subject to discrimination at the hands of the voters. The strength of the work and the resulting conclusion on voter treatment of women is that the finding has been made consistently, with reliable and appropriate data. Use of a nearly limitless supply of Election Day returns has led these studies, examining different levels of office, different times, and different places, to the same conclusion; women are not discriminated against at the ballot box.

The few studies that do assert that women are subject to differential treatment from the voters do not claim that such bias is widespread. On the contrary, such bias is only visible in isolated instances (Werner 1993; Sigelman, Thomas, Sigelman, and Ribich 1986; Byrne and Pueschel 1974). Thus the evidence is that voters are not biased against women, and where bias does appear it is not found to be common, but evinced rarely.

Although most studies have failed to detect any outward bias against women, other researchers have questioned whether bias might operate at a more subtle level. For example, the relatively low information amounts typically available to voters might force them to make inferences about candidates (Rapoport, Metcalf, and Hartman 1989). Inferences concerning candidate competence, leadership ability, and integrity have been shown to be produced when a voter merely views a picture of a candidate (Sigelman, Sigelman, and Fowler 1987; Rosenberg, Bohan, McCafferty, and Harris 1986). If a picture can produce inferences, one would think that knowledge of candidate gender would as well.

Experiments and survey work on reactions to female candidates have found that when information is sparse (for example, when the candidate is a challenger running for the first time), gender powerfully informs the assumptions people make (Alexander and Andersen 1993; Dayhoff 1983). Unfortunately, the assumptions made with little information do not tend to favor women (Huddy and Terkildsen 1993a, 1993b; Alexander and Andersen 1993; Perkins and Fowlkes 1980). With little else to go on, voters fall back on stereotypes of women as less decisive or less competent (Alexander and Andersen 1993; Gitelson and Gitelson 1981). These stereotypes must be overcome by the woman candidate, a task male candidates do not have to face. Fortunately, as more information is gained, the evaluation of women candidates becomes more reliant on the actual candidate rather than stereotypes (Sapiro 1981b; Alexander and Andersen 1993). To wit, simply providing the fact that a woman candidate won an election tends to transform respondents' thinking away from gender and toward their thoughts about successful politicians (Gitelson and Gitelson 1981).

It is important to note that these biased inferences did not produce significant bias in vote choice. However, if the subjects and voters in these studies were capable of making some biased inferences about women, one would think elites may fall prey to similar biases. Elites, however, play a magnified role in the process--not merely choosing the better of two candidates--but navigating through a river full of potential candidates.

Contributors

In addition to voters, another key arbiter of demand for women candidates are those who contribute money to candidates. Studies of legislative races have concluded that the three key variables in such contests are incumbency, party, and money (Moncrief 1992; Tucker and Weber 1987; Caldeira and Patterson 1982a, 1982b; Tucker 1986; Giles and Pritchard 1985; Gierzynski and Breaux 1991; Breaux and Gierzynski 1991; Welch 1976). Given the fact that a prospective female candidate is in no position to alter her party or her incumbency status, the dynamic variable is money. Money thus becomes a focus for those seeking to explain the electoral success patterns of women candidates.

Since women have historically fared better in states with less-populated districts (Diamond 1977), many have assumed the decreased need for money in such districts to be a large factor in that trend (Werner 1968; Mandel 1981). Evidence to the contrary, however, abounds. Scholars examining congressional and state legislative candidate fundraising have found no bias against females when party and incumbency are controlled (Darcy, Welch, and Clark 1994; Herrick 1995; Harrison 1995; Werner 1993; McLean 1994; Biersack and Herrnson 1994; Benze and Declercq 1985; Burrell 1993, 1994a; Wilhite and Theilman 1987; Uhlaner and Schlozman 1986). Meanwhile, others who have examined state legislative campaigns have found that, increasingly, the only variable of significance in fundraising is the competitiveness of the district (Werner 1993; Thompson, Cassie, and Jewell 1994; Jones and Borris 1985; Stonecash 1988; Dwyre and Stonecash 1992). Thus, candidates running in open-seats or in very competitive districts attract large sums of money, frequently from their party's legislative committee campaign fund (Gierzynski 1992). For women, this means that it is not likely that they will suffer from under-funding if they are in a competitive race. However, women are often challengers facing long electoral odds, which means that money will be exceedingly hard to come by--not because they are women, but because the money is targeted for the closest races.

Even without any gender bias, it is very hard for a challenger to raise the money necessary to overcome the power of incumbency (Moncrief and Thompson 1995; Giles and Pritchard 1985). One of the most obvious and relevant facts of American politics is that incumbents tend to win re-election. If the vast majority of legislators are male in one session, one would expect that this would remain true in the next session. Alarmingly, for those interested in seeing women elected, the turnover rate in state legislatures has been dropping over the last 40 years (Niemi and Winsky 1987; Shin and Jackson 1979; Rosenthal 1974). Moreover, the average margin of victory for incumbent legislative candidates is growing (Jewell and Breaux 1988). According to some scholars, the single most daunting obstacle for the election of women is simply the inertia built into the system which we call incumbency advantage (Andersen and Thorson 1984; Darcy and Choike 1986). All this could lead one to conclude that the problem with the under-representation of women boils down to the fact that men won the seats first, and the men have chosen to keep them. A closer examination reveals that the story is not as simple.

THE CANDIDACY DECISION

Despite the plethora of successful incumbents, there are, of course, legislators who decide to retire. These open-seat races tend to be very competitive since the lack of an incumbent frequently means that either side has a realistic chance to win. The distribution of open-seat candidacies is so crucial that it has been identified by some as the key to women's representation at the state legislative level (Carroll 1994; Ambrosius and Welch 1984). It is in the relationship between challenger and open-seat candidacies that a stark difference emerges between male and female candidates. Some scholars have found that female candidates are disproportionately likely to win nominations to run as longshot challengers and disproportionately unlikely to run as open-seat nominees (in state legislatures: Diamond 1977; Carroll and Strimling 1983; Werner 1993; in Congress: Burrell 1988). This is certainly a curious pattern since there is no obvious reason for women to wish to run only in more difficult elections.

One explanation for this pattern could be that women are less qualified and knowledgeable candidates than men, and therefore they choose to run in longshot races. This notion loses credence because national and state-based analyses of male and female candidates show that women and men candidates have similar economic and social backgrounds (Kirkpatrick 1974; Diamond 1977), have similar reasons for pursuing office (McLean 1994), have comparable political qualifications (Gaddie and Bullock 1995; Carroll 1994; McLean 1994; Burrell 1994a), use similar campaign tactics (Procter, Schenck-Hamlin, and Haase 1994; Mezey 1978a), emphasize similar issues (Carroll 1994; Mezey 1978b), put forth similar effort (Studlar and McAllister 1991), and even achieve similar results with regard to campaign exposure, issue congruence, and evaluation by the voters (Darcy, Welch, and Clark 1994).

If women are essentially equal to men in political standing as candidates, then it is unlikely that gender causes female candidates to seek tougher races. Moreover, national surveys of female candidates show that the vast majority of legislative candidates were recruited to run for the state legislature by party officials (Carroll 1994; Diamond 1977), and that women show no greater predilection for self-started campaigns than men (McLean 1994; Carroll and Strimling 1983). The tendency for women to run in hopeless races, coupled with the fact that most women are recruited, suggests that the culprits in this situation might be members of the political elite who recruit candidates for legislative office (Burrell 1993; Lamson 1968).

Elite/Potential Candidate Interaction

Candidates do not decide whether to run in a vacuum (Fowler 1979, 1993; Canon, Schousen, and Sellers 1994; Abel and Oppenheimer 1994; Seligman 1961).

In the traditional conception of political contests, there are two groups at the first gate--elites and prospective candidates. Systematic study has indicated that party elites play an important role in state legislative elections by encouraging candidacies (McLean 1994; Frendreis, Gibson, and Vertz 1990). How potential candidates and party elites interact to produce active candidates thus shapes the campaigns, voter decisions, and eventually the winning officeholders (Frendreis and Gitelson, 1995; Werner 1993). Broadly, the process of candidate emergence is therefore of fundamental importance to democratic theory (Kazee 1994b; Hertzke 1994).

Although elites cannot guarantee a nomination to a recruited candidate, the importance of their role in candidate emergence should not be underestimated because well over half of all state legislative seat nominations go uncontested (Frendreis and Gitelson 1995; Grau 1981). This, coupled with the fact that there are more "one-party districts" on the state legislative level than for Congress, suggests the importance of party elites in state legislative candidate decisions (Frendreis and Gitelson 1995).

On the congressional level, a number of studies illustrate the capacity of county parties to, if not directly secure, at least build the foundation of party nominations (Fowler and McClure 1989; Canon, Schousen, and Sellers 1994; Abel and Oppenheimer 1994; Herrnson and Tennant 1994; Hertzke 1994; Kazee and Roberts 1994). In many cases this is accomplished by successfully discouraging weaker or disliked candidates from running (Fowler and McClure 1989). Even when elites are not explicitly asking someone to run, they have usually spent time grooming candidates and helping them to be in a position to emerge when openings occurred (Kazee and Thornberry 1990). Party leaders have many different levels on which to exercise their influence: direct contact with prospective candidates, trading of political favors with other interested people, organization of party loyalists, and strategic mentions of prospective candidates to the media (Fowler and McClure 1989; Canon, Schousen, and Sellers 1994; Abel and Oppenheimer 1994; Herrnson and Tennant 1994; Hertzke 1994; Kazee and Roberts 1994).

Obviously, if elites influence who decides to run, elites then help determine who wins. Hunt and Pendley (1972) assess the import of recruitment, "The results of this study indicate the existence of an independent structure of political actors in the community who, through their choice of who to promote to sponsored candidacy, translate implicit and vague community norms and values into concrete responses to the recurrent question of who shall govern" (437). Concomitantly, Pomper (1965, 197) refers to county party chairs as "the means of articulation" between the electorate and government. Elites' abilities to share political "intelligence" and to create a political buzz can help shape the public's perception of political reality (Fowler and McClure 1989). Additionally, elite endorsements and participation in the campaigns of such candidates are two of the few significant determinants of success in down-ballot races (Howell and Oiler 1981; Werner 1993; Sheffield and Goering 1978).

Since most research has failed to document significant voter bias against women, many analysts argue that the key to gaining more female officeholders is simply to field more women candidates (Burrell 1988, 1992, 1994a; Norris and Lovenduski 1993). In his analysis of candidate emergence, Kazee (1994a) presents a list of six factors that affect the decision to run. While most of the factors would not contribute to an explanation of the paucity of women candidates, one that might is access. Access, in the form of a favorable reception from their party, places a limit on the types of candidates who are likely to succeed quite separate from their interest or ability to run. Put simply, if the party elites can influence prospective candidate behavior, then they can influence (limit) the number of women who run and in turn influence (limit) the number of women who hold office.

Elite behavior is of great importance because of their role in a process that begins with many people who can appear objectively similar and ends with a tiny fraction of them taking an active role in politics. Elite efforts to activate individuals into politics can determine who participates and who remains unheard (Bowman and Boynton 1971). Initial political activity seems to hinge on the efforts of elites to open the door for some of the many waiting outside (Rosenstone and Hansen 1993). Not only do many individual women need the encouragement of elites to become active (Burrell 1988; Frazier 1993), but some research suggests that women tend to be more dependent on external validation (Messe and Watts 1980) and would therefore be more reluctant than men to presume that they belong in politics without an invitation.

Fowler and McClure (1989) relate anecdotal evidence supporting the assertion that prospective women candidates are more reliant on external validation of their political merit. Louise Slaughter, considering a run for Congress, was apprehensive about her chances despite her experience, connections, and a favorable climate. In 1984, in an open-seat race, and in 1986, in a contest with a one-term incumbent, Slaughter sought expensive poll results that would indicate her prospects before she would acknowledge her strengths in the district. She also sought assurances from both local and national party figures that she would receive adequate support. When her reception was quite warm, but not overwhelming, she decided to stay out of the 1984 race. In 1986, with polls and party elites supporting her again, she entered the contest and eventually defeated the incumbent. In sum, Louise Slaughter would run only with copious external evidence of her value as a candidate. This anecdotal generalization is borne out in McLean's (1994) survey data, which show women to be more reliant on encouragement from others in deciding whether to run for office. McLean also finds that women considering a run for higher office are more concerned with established viability (by polls) and prospective party support.

UNBIASED ELITES?

Clearly the political elite would be expected to seek candidates on the basis of their likelihood of victory, sometimes going as far as compiling a profile of the hypothetical ideal candidate (Hertzke 1994; Haskell, Sutten, and Squire 1994). These educated, experienced, professional individuals would not be expected to fall prey to biases since they have both the knowledge and the motivation to avoid prejudice. By definition, elite party leaders would be expected to follow election results very closely. Given that the vast thrust of evidence, both in popular journalistic and scholarly sources, is that women are not discriminated against at the polls, one would expect that elites would act on this information because it is simply in their best interest to encourage the best candidates they can (Darcy, Welch, and Clark 1994).

Some researchers have concluded that elites do not, in fact, display bias in their behavior. McDonald and Pierson (1984) compile a survey of female elites in which there is little reported discrimination inhibiting women's progress. Unfortunately, the study was restricted to successful candidates and party chairs, not precisely the groups one would expect to have suffered the most discrimination. A far more interesting, and socially significant, picture would develop if women who were unable to win office, unable to secure a party position, or gave up trying were asked about their experiences with elite bias (Kazee 1994a).

Darcy, Welch, and Clark (1994) also claim to show that elites are not biased against women. They conclude that there is "no evidence of a male conspiracy" (184). However, Darcy, Welch, and Clark admit earlier in their work that "Even if there were a male conspiracy, it would be very difficult to document directly" (69). While their use of the phrase "male conspiracy" almost suggests that they are looking to find meetings of secret societies organized to stifle the political involvement of women, in fact, Darcy, Welch, and Clark do not attempt to directly examine the behavior of party leaders; nor do they examine the behavior of potential women candidates. Instead, their conclusions are based on evidence gleaned only from the treatment of nominated candidates. For example, Darcy, Welch, and Clark utilize campaign contributions to nominated female candidates. One problem with this as a proxy for party leader treatment of women is that it assumes that party elites control all the money. More importantly, this measure is of only tangential concern if the elite are in any way limiting the number of women running. Thus, Darcy, Welch, and Clark, despite their conclusion that elites are not biased, have no evidence concerning the treatment of the key group, potential women candidates.

McLean (1994) conducted a national survey of officeholding men and women and asked them a battery of questions dealing with their electoral experiences. McLean finds that male and female officeholders at various levels (local, state, national) received the same amount of support from their parties. Among her conclusions, she argues her data show that if gender significantly affects political careers, it does so after officeholders reach the state legislative level. More dramatically, she claims, "These findings challenge arguments that political parties are more likely to recruit and support male candidates rather than female candidates to run for public office" (143).

McLean admits that she has no data on the effort expended by these men and women to secure equal treatment from the parties, therefore women or men could have to work harder to receive equal treatment. Unfortunately, this is not the most serious limitation of McLean's evidence. More damagingly, the methods employed by McLean do not lend credibility to either of the two conclusions mentioned. First, McLean's sample of both men and women is primarily made up of those who have successfully attained state legislative office. Equality of result through the state legislative level is not an indication of reality but primarily a result of the lack of variation in the sample. Moreover, equality of treatment by political parties is again demonstrated in these data by examining the treatment of successful candidates. By systematically excluding those most likely to have been mistreated by parties, McLean's belief that she challenges arguments that political parties are biased is overstated.

After pointing out the deficiencies in others' work, including that of Darcy (Darcy and Schramm 1977), whose conclusion on elite treatment of women she downgrades into "only an assertion," Burrell (1994a, 83) presents data purporting to show that parties are no longer negative forces against women. In fact, she boldly claims "notions of prejudice [in the political system] are passe" (191). She bases this conclusion on party money donations, which she claims is the only type of data that reveal the involvement of parties in the process.

Unfortunately, Burrell's assumption that parties play no role in the decisions of prospective candidates seems exaggerated given the pattern of findings revealed in numerous studies that provide in-depth examination of parties and candidates in congressional districts. Rather than playing no role in candidate decisions, parties encouraged and discouraged countless candidates from running and worked hard to secure nominations for the chosen candidates (Fowler and McClure 1989; Kazee and Thornberry 1990; Canon, Schousen, and Sellers 1994; Abel and Oppenheimer 1994; Herrnson and Tennant 1994; Hertzke 1994; Kazee and Roberts 1994).

Moreover, that Burrell's conception of the process includes only party money (which is given only to nominees) also demonstrates the limits of her conclusion. It is not that the parties are above bias toward women; more accurately she shows (just as Darcy, Welch, and Clark did) that the parties are above financial bias against nominated women.[?]

Properly qualified, the work of Burrell, Darcy and colleagues, McLean, and McDonald and Pierson makes a significant contribution. Their results are quite informative regarding the treatment of nominated and elected women. By examining contributions and the reports of treatment received by these women, these scholars have built a credible case that nominated and elected women are not subject to biased treatment from political elites. This is an important conclusion with significant implications for the task of maintaining women's presence in elected office. However, due to the nature of the research designs employed, none of these studies should claim that their results inform us with regard to the overall treatment of women by party elites, nor specifically with regard to the treatment of potential women candidates.

Obviously, the failure to document bias (in some situations) is not evidence of a fair system. Research should go beyond the evidence gathered by these scholars to directly examine the behavior of all the relevant actors (Werner 1993). As Norris and Lovenduski (1993, 382) argue, we must attend to the "discouraged aspirants," those whose names never emerge on a ballot because their ambitions were stymied earlier in the process. Unfortunately, the work and conclusions of Darcy and his colleagues, McDonald and Pierson, McLean, and Burrell fails to consider the plight of discouraged aspirants. Thus, all their conclusions regarding bias must be dealt with cautiously. As a consequence of the failure to examine discouraged aspirants, we know very little about the scope of elite bias and its ramifications, specifically concerning its effects on the number of women who decide to pursue office. Studies claiming that we can conclude that there is little elite bias against women candidates without any direct examination of potential women candidates or of party recruiters would be akin to an accountant proclaiming a company to be in good fiscal health by looking at the physical output of the company without knowing how its money was spent. With this perspective, we can see only the output, not the processes, corrupt or otherwise, that produced the output.

THE ARGUMENT FOR ELITE BIAS

Contrary to the conclusions of Darcy, Welch, and Clark, McLean, Burrell, and McDonald and Pierson, patterns of elite behavior suggest that female candidates may suffer from bias harbored by party leaders (Werner 1993; Main, Gryski, and Shapiro 1984). The inclination to assume that knowledgeable party leaders are above perceptual bias is challenged by research conducted outside the realm of party politics that suggests the possibility that elites are sometimes biased against women. Ferber, Huber, and Spitze (1979) show a preference for male professionals among a wide array of people, including the highly educated. Dipboye, Fromkin, and Wiback (1975) find a tendency among both personnel people and college students to judge male job candidates higher than female candidates. Stivers (1993) finds that government leaders seek job applicants with characteristics associated with white men. These are all situations where one would expect that in the effort to find the best person, unjustified bias would be ignored in lieu of meaningful evidence.

Despite that expectation, some research has found ingroup favoritism is perpetuated even when such behavior is disadvantageous for the ingroup (Brown, Collins, and Schmidt 1988; Turner, Brown, and Tajfel 1979). Beyond self-interest, many would imagine that education and expertise would deter people from falling prey to perceptual bias. Jackman, however, has argued that education and position do not liberate people from intergroup negativism (Jackman and Muha 1984). In fact, education can bolster bias; when you believe yourself to be knowledgeable about something, you can more easily convince yourself that your decisions are based on expertise, not prejudice. Jussim (1990) argues that those with high belief certainty have a low accuracy motivation because when they believe they are right they do not invest much effort in seeking objective confirmation. According to Jackman, instead of lifting people beyond bias, education primarily enables people to adopt an outlook that protects their interests. When party leaders are presented a potential female candidate, if their instincts tell them she would not make a good candidate, they could immediately assume that their decision is based on political knowledge and give the situation little further thought. This explanation is also in keeping with research that suggests that women are often the victims of hidden prejudice, which originates in non-conscious beliefs, but has the ultimate effect of keeping women from advancing (Bem and Bem 1970).

This hidden prejudice may have its influence in the form of expectancy effects. Snyder argues that "Events in the social world may be as much effects of individuals' beliefs as they are causes of these beliefs" (1984, 294). In other words, the expectation that someone (a woman candidate) will perform poorly will lead to different treatment by the perceiver (the party leader) which can then negatively alter the woman's performance, and ultimately result in a negative evaluation (Harris 1990; Jussim 1990).

Expectancy effects are more likely to occur when the perceiver must evaluate ambiguous information (Jussim 1990) such as the quality of a person's ideas, which is obviously going to happen when considering someone for a political run. One of the main criteria recruiters use is interpersonal skills (Prewitt 1970), which must be based on subjective, somewhat ambiguous information. Fowler and McClure (1989) find that many potential candidates appeared similar with regard to objective qualifications, yet had to be sorted out by recruiters. Eventually, subjective or ambiguous qualities had to be relied upon to evaluate the field. Alarmingly, Eagly, Makhijani, and Klonsky (1992) find that women are subject to a noticeable bias in the evaluation of leadership skills when the judgment is based on ambiguous information. Not only do studies tend to find a pro-male bias in expectancy effects (Jussim and Eccles 1992), but the expectancy effect process is further magnified because women tend to react more negatively to being negatively perceived than do men (Harris 1990).

Lest this be exaggerated, the expectancy effect process is most likely to occur when the perceiver has the least information. Therefore, the target of evaluation, given adequate time, can generally overcome this bias. Unfortunately, where opportunity is limited and potential candidates are plentiful (which could occur at a candidate screening meeting), there may not be enough time for an interviewer to make more than an initial meeting and judgment.[3]

Absent direct evidence on the political elite, Jackman's theory sounds like an attractive explanation for the behavior of party leaders. It becomes even more applicable when one considers that Jackman's argument predicts that the educated will attempt to quell disturbances from the weaker group by placating rather than fighting or making meaningful change. This sounds suspiciously like political elites channeling women into hopeless races, which prevents women from arguing that they are totally shut out while at the same time keeping them from attaining any real power.

Using a survey of politically active women, Van Hightower (1977) found that most of the women who had *run for office* had been recruited by leaders of their political party. However, most women who had actually *won office* decided to run on their own (see also Miller 1986). Carroll's (1994) national survey of female legislative candidates shows that the more time and effort put into recruiting a prospective woman candidate, the more likely the race is against a strong incumbent. It appears that women are frequently recruited as sacrificial lambs, meant to fill space on the ballot rather than actually win office (Werner 1993; Gertzog and Simard 1981; Deber 1982; Bernstein 1986).

Werner (1993, 246), in his four-state study on women's candidacies, concludes that elite bias is "detectable and not insignificant." To simplify his analysis, Werner labeled all county parties as having either a strong organization or a weak organization. He then assumed that strong organizations recruit all their candidates while weak organizations recruit none of their candidates. If these assumptions were plausible, and he then found that conditions were less favorable for women in strong party areas, he could conclude that parties with power were biased against women. Indeed, Werner finds that women are less likely to secure open-seat nominations and more likely to run in hopeless races in strong party areas.

One obvious problem with this effort is the assumption that strong parties recruit all their candidates and weak parties none. Certainly, some candidates run and win in strong party areas without being recruited, while even the weakest party may recruit some candidates (Gibson, Frendreis, and Vertz 1989). Werner makes too much out of a dichotomous variable that was not designed to perfectly predict recruiting efforts (see Gibson, Frendreis, and Vertz 1989). Moreover, given that strong party organizations tend to spring up in more competitive electoral areas (Gibson, Frendreis, and Vertz 1989), one has to worry that perhaps Werner's findings are spurious, and that it is not party organization that influences the number of women but the competitiveness of the two parties. Werner does attempt to control for public opinion by including an estimated measure of public support for women's political activity. Werner finds that strong party districts with hostile public opinion are the least conducive to women's electoral efforts. While Werner argues this is evidence of a mass bias against women, he is again unable to rule out plausible counter explanations. Vandenbosch (1995) is left with a similar problem when she finds an inverse relationship between the number of Christians and the number of women candidates. Neither can determine whether it is really the mass opinion that is stymieing women who want to run, or if the women themselves share the same opinions and therefore avoid politics.

Werner's conclusions are based on inferences made by examining the number of women seeking and winning office in various conditions. Werner has no direct data concerning the decision-making process of either party leaders or prospective women candidates, and therefore cannot respond to the challenge that perhaps it is lack of desire to run on the part of women, or competitiveness, rather than strong party bias, that is at work here. Finally, despite his persuasive argument that too much work on women's candidacies has failed to examine individual level processes, Werner himself has failed to shed light on individual-level decision making. Most glaringly, even if we accept Werner's conclusion that there is elite bias against women, his data shed no light on the question of the origins of bias. Whether such bias is rooted in the elite's personal prejudice, or whether the bias reflects no personal animus on the part of the elite but instead is a product of the elite's opinion of the electorate's prejudice, cannot be distinguished.

After acknowledging the limitations of Werner's data, his conclusion that women seem to be less likely to secure open-seat nominations nevertheless remains important. In the distribution of open-seat races, as in many other situations for women, their interests are acceptable at the periphery (Bem and Bem 1970) or, as Millett (1971, 62) puts it, "Women are a dependency class who live on surplus." Instead of running in contests with equal chances of winning, according to Werner, women tend to find themselves discouraged from pursuing the most attractive races.

ELECTORAL STRUCTURE AND BIAS

In defense of elites, alternate explanations for the lack of women legislators have been suggested, such as structural variables that have been linked to the number of women in state legislatures. Multi-member districts (Moncrief and Thompson 1992; Matland and Brown 1992; Werner 1968; Diamond 1977; Darcy, Welch, and Clark 1985, 1994; Rule 1987, 1990; Carroll 1994; Clark, Darcy, Welch, and Ambrosius 1984) and small population districts (Diamond 1977; Werner 1968; Rule 1981) have been shown to be strongly related to higher levels of female representation. Given the lack of evidence of voter discrimination and the lack of evidence of financial bias against women candidates, however, the most plausible explanation of this pattern is simply that elites are less selective in finding candidates in areas where they need multiple candidates (Diamond 1977). Diamond utilizes the examples of the legislatures of Arizona and Connecticut in the 1970s, when both states lowered the number of legislative seats (increasing the population per seat) but did not disproportionately lose women legislators (Fowlkes [1984a] documents the same process in Georgia; see also Bullock and MacManus 1991). Despite a less advantageous structure, the number of women remained stable, suggesting that it is not something inherent in the structure that influences female representation. Toward that end, Studlar and Welch (1991) find that the relationship between number of women elected and number of seats per district is not linear. Werner (1993) argues that systems are not biased or favorable for women, but that different systems mitigate or accentuate the bias of individuals.

Rule (1987) and Darcy, Welch, and Clark (1994) outline the advantage for women under a multi-member district system. Instead of having a party group organized around each seat, as would exist with a single member district, multi-member districts encourage fewer groups organized around a number of seats. Since they are contesting more than one seat, allowing a woman to run is less of a sacrifice than giving your one space on the ballot to a woman. Further, having a number of seats may create some accountability, as women in the party are likely to be less tolerant of not getting a single space on the ballot when there are many than when there is one. Again, rather than the structure itself, the phenomenon of women's representation in multi-member districts suggests that elite reaction to the system may be the cause of the difference.

Despite the great effort put forth by many scholars in examining the connection between structure and number of women, the work is largely abandoned after the initial connection is established. The real origin of the connection lies in unexamined individuals' behavior (Werner 1993). To really understand factors influencing women, individual behavior cannot be ignored.

Whatever the link between structure and women, it is clear that the number of women in office changes, sometimes dramatically, every election. An adequate explanation of the number of elected women must allow for rapid change. Structural variables are, of course, relatively inert. Such rapid change could exist, however, in the turnover of party officials and in the changing political assessments of such officials.

 Carroll (1994) describes the party leader as a victim of cross-pressures. Party leaders simultaneously want to maintain their position, to please others in their party, to have women contribute to the party's efforts, and to field candidates who have the best chances of winning. If a party leader (for whatever reason) believes a woman is less likely to win, then there is great pressure on that individual to balance the value of women's participation with the value of winning. An attractive compromise would be to discourage women from running in competitive races, but to encourage women to run in hopeless races, where it does not matter how good the candidate is because loss is likely and where one can show that women have not been totally ignored in the process. Such a scheme would "simultaneously exclude women and obfuscate the perception of exclusion" (Werner 1993, 128).

If party elites are important in the process, and if they are displaying bias against women, the obvious question is why. Why would political party elites consider women inferior candidates? Why would elites discourage women from running or channel their talents and efforts into unwinnable races? Moreover, one must wonder what effect such bias has on women's candidacy decisions. Exploring these questions will be the task of this research, the plan for which is presented in the next chapter.

SUMMARY

When examining the lack of women in state legislatures, the blame could be directed at the attitudes of women, the attitudes of voters and contributors, or the attitudes of the elite candidate recruiters. Evidence indicates, however, that neither potential women candidates' behavior nor the voters' or contributors' preferences provide sufficient explanation for the dearth of women legislators.

The role of elite recruiters and their interaction with potential women candidates is both less studied and less clear. Party leaders are capable of retarding the growth of the number of women in state legislatures (Carroll 1994) because the number of women in office depends upon the number of women who run and the number of women who run in realistic races. Since the vast majority of candidates are recruited to run, party leaders are in a position to influence both numbers (Carroll 1994; Frazier 1993; Diamond 1977; Rule 1981). For many analysts, the paucity of women winners is primarily a consequence of the lack of women candidates (Burrell 1988, 1992, 1994a; Norris and Lovenduski 1993; Gaddie and Bullock 1995). McLean's (1994) national survey of officeholders finds that, once elected to the office of their choice, men and women receive substantially similar treatment from their parties. This supports the notion that the recruitment of prospective candidates is the crucial step where women are either invited to join as full members or stymied. Moreover, the start of a political career is when talents are most in doubt--where women suffer the greatest differential in need to be recruited (McLean 1994). With that in mind, women and politics scholars have called for a greater understanding of recruitment (Carroll 1994; Darcy and Schramm 1977; Rule 1981; Clark, Hadley, and Darcy 1989; Rosenwasser et al. 1987; Akins 1996).

While other factors may contribute to the paucity of women legislators, ignoring the role of elites leaves us with an insufficient understanding of the process. To wit, Burrell (1988) has emphatically stated, "The importance of exploring the recruitment process cannot be overemphasized" (67).

NOTES

1. Fowler and McClure (1989), in their study of one New York congressional district, document the case of a successful Republican woman who was encouraged to run for the State Senate, but who met with a chilly reception from the party when the idea of her running for Congress was broached. The woman abandoned the idea of running for Congress and happily pursued the state legislature. She, like most other politicians examined in the study, expressed a great deal of fondness for service in the state legislature (for among other reasons a nice salary and less family disruption than in higher office). The lack of an ambition gap or the widespread positive value of state legislative work among both men and women, however, brings us no closer to understanding the gender imbalance in state legislatures.

2. Biersack and Herrnson (1994), also using financial contributions, come to the same conclusion. They state emphatically that the "road to Congress is not blocked by arbitrary bias by the political parties" (178).

3. Which Dipboye, Fromkin, and Wiback (1975) warn frequently occurs in the business world.

3

An Exploration of Elite Bias

If elite bias exists, the obvious question is: Why would a party leader surmise that a woman is an inferior candidate? This is especially perplexing in a time when women are widely seen as outsiders, more capable of connecting to a cynical electorate (Hertzke 1994; Haskell, Sutten, and Squire 1994; Burrell 1993; Delli Carpini and Fuchs 1993), and when national surveys report a majority of Americans believe we would be better off if women held half of all government offices. This chapter offers, first, a review of two forms of perceptual effects (the outgroup effect and the distribution effect) that might influence elite behavior and create bias against women. Second, this chapter presents the research design with which the forms, origins, and effects of bias will be explored.

The two possible forms of bias feature an important distinction between the origins of perceptual bias. In the outgroup explanation, it is the male party leader who is more comfortable with the male candidate because of their surface similarity to each other, and who therefore sees the male candidate as more capable. In the distribution explanation, the party leader is surveying the political landscape and making more of a statistical conclusion based on the genderized division of labor. This results in women being penalized because of the association of higher-status occupations with men and the greater prevalence of men in elected office. In essence, the outgroup effect penalizes those who do not look like the evaluator, while the distribution effect penalizes those who do not look like the previously successful.

In either case, if elite party recruiters think women candidates are less attractive or less likely to win, then party leaders could discourage them from running or channel them into hopeless races. This is not to suggest that all party leaders are biased against women, or that those who are biased will favor men in perpetuity.

Studies have shown that with enough information on traits and characteristics, the informative power of gender shrinks (Eagly and Steffen 1984; Deaux and Lewis 1984). However, it is important to realize that judgments of political worth can begin at first sight (Sigelman, Sigelman, and Fowler 1987; Rosenberg et al. 1986), and that party leaders who fall prey to bias at an early stage may not pursue the information necessary to properly assess a potential female candidate.

THE OUTGROUP EFFECT

Why would party elites react negatively to female candidates? One potential answer begins with the fact that most party leaders are men. For male party leaders, assumptions regarding females translate into assumptions involving an outgroup. Psychologists find members of the outgroup are frequently lumped together in a person's mind, such that qualities associated with the group are associated with all the individual members of that group (Jones, Wood, and Quattrone 1981; Judd and Park 1988; Mackie and Worth 1989; Carpenter 1993). If a male party leader holds the view that most women are not as politically inclined as men, one would expect that prospective female candidates would be lumped into an outgroup in which the default assumption is that a woman is not as politically capable as a man. Outgrouping inhibits individuation, which by definition limits the ability of the qualified woman to distinguish herself from the party leader's notion of women in general. This tendency to see members of the outgroup as less heterogenous has been demonstrated to be stronger in competitive situations (Judd and Park 1988), which certainly characterizes efforts to secure party nominations. When confronted with a woman who wants to run for office, the elite's perception of women will likely lead the elite to either encourage the woman not to run or possibly to encourage her to run in a hopeless race where her candidacy will do little damage.

Meanwhile, if party leaders see potential male candidates as part of the ingroup, they are likely to individually evaluate the person. Moreover, ingroup members are generally assumed to be similar to the perceiver in attitudes, values, and personality (Piliavin 1987). This assumption of similarity can be very significant when a subjective evaluation must be made, as similarity induces assumptions of competence (Klahr 1969). In essence, ingroup members are inclined to positively evaluate fellow ingroup members and to always give ingroup members the opportunity to demonstrate their valued qualities.

Outgroup members are also subject to polarization effects. In simple terms, the weight of positive and negative information on an outgroup member tends to be exaggerated (Linville and Jones 1980). If an outgroup member is actually thought to have some positive attribute, the value of that information is magnified to far greater importance than similar information on an ingroup member. This has the practical effect of allowing an observer to maintain negative assessments of the outgroup as a whole while acknowledging the undeniable traits of one particular group member. Meanwhile, when negative attributes are associated with an outgroup member, this information is also exaggerated, as it serves the purpose of confirming ingroup members' suspicions about the traits and tendencies of the outgroup.

The tendency to polarize outgroup information suggests that successful women candidates will be viewed as very strong candidates who are in no way typical of the capabilities of other women. Unsuccessful women, however, will not only see their failures exaggerated, but their performance will likely be associated with, and thought indicative of, other women's limitations.

The tendency to make positive assumptions about ingroup members but not outgroup members, the tendency to homogenize the outgroup without regard to the attributes of the individual, and the tendency to exaggerate traits of the outgroup rather than recognize the information in proportion to its weight (or the weight it would have if it referred to an ingroup member) are all components of the outgroup effect. Inherent in these processes are advantages for ingroup members and disadvantages for outgroup members when approval is sought.

Studies have found outgroup bias operating in countless situations including such significant, real-world settings as school boards choosing a superintendent (Marietti 1992). Given the breadth of the findings, it is not surprising that political examples exist. One study of male and female state legislators suggests that female candidates may suffer from the effects of outgroup bias. Dubeck (1976) found that younger, less experienced men were encouraged to run, while only women with extensive party experience and a strong background were acceptable as candidates (see also Studlar and McAllister 1991; Mezey 1980). In a sense, males were judged based on their potential; party leaders tended to search for information that made the male seem an attractive candidate. Females, on the other hand, were extended no credit for potential. Females tended to have much less opportunity to sell themselves as future candidates and tended to be dismissed much more quickly than men. Margolis (1980) even found that women in the local parties she studied were not acknowledged to have done nearly as much work as they had performed, while male party workers were subject to no such under-count.

Another example of an ingroup preference among elite party members was demonstrated in Patterson and Boynton's (1970) study of the political structure in Iowa in the late 1960s. They found that while one could easily distinguish between the characteristics of the elite group and the mass electorate, the homogeneity within the elite group was pervasive. Extending from party leaders to legislators, the demographic and opinion similarity was quite strong. The absence of identifiable traits or characteristics that could distinguish the party elite from the officeholders suggests that party elites might have searched for candidates to run based on the candidates' similarity to themselves (see also Norris and Lovenduski 1993). Toward that end, Yount (1986) argues that people are more comfortable around those who are similar to themselves but become more easily bored and uncomfortable with dissimilar others.

Prewitt (1970) and Hunt and Pendley (1972) assert that this situation figures in recruitment. Prewitt argues that since the recruiter is quite possibly launching someone on a career path in which their influence will eclipse that of the recruiter, there is great concern that the new candidate be like the recruiter. This similarity is used as a shortcut to ensure both appropriate values and temperament for the job. Hunt and Pendley find that the recruiting person or group is very concerned about future relations between the new candidate and the recruiters, and therefore their assessment of how they will get along with the new candidate is of utmost importance. Again, similarity is used as a means of testing how the candidate will relate to the group in the future.

THE DISTRIBUTION EFFECT

An alternate explanation for elite bias is the distribution effect, where the differential distribution into productive roles feeds the perception of gender-based differences (Eagly and Wood 1982). Because of sexual segregation in work roles, men outnumber women in positions of achievement and women more frequently have low-status jobs. This results in abstractions of the sexes based on their distribution in productive roles (Yount 1986; Kiesler 1975; Eagly and Wood 1982). Eagly and Wood emphasize that this does not mean that people judge men to be inherently superior; men in low-status jobs, for example, are not thought of as more capable than women in high-status jobs. The danger lies in the initial assumptions people make, which without contradicting information will result in men being viewed more favorably because of the status associated with men in the work force (Eagly and Mladinic 1989).

In addition to assumptions based on the division of productive roles, another aspect of the distribution effect is the salience of the numerically rare. When one encounters a female in an occupation area dominated by males, the incongruity feeds doubts concerning the appropriateness of the woman's position (Eagly, Makhijani, and Klonsky 1992).

The distribution effect would occur in politics because women are more likely than men to pursue home-based or low-status work and because women officeholders are comparatively rare. Therefore, party leaders encountering a woman interested in political office could subconsciously assume that men are more likely to succeed in politics. This assumption colors their behavior, not because they view women as inherently incapable, but because their understanding of the political landscape (the distribution of gender among officeholders) leads them to believe men are more likely to succeed.

To explore gender-based inferences, Sapiro (1981b) and Leeper (1991) both utilized an experimental design in which subjects read a political speech that was either identified as having been given by a female candidate or a male candidate. Both studies generally found that neither understanding nor favorability toward the speech was affected by the gender manipulation.

Significantly, both studies also found that the male speaker was thought more likely to win his hypothetical race than the female to win her hypothetical race (see also Rosenwasser and Dean 1989). This difference was present in the responses of both male and female subjects. This pattern fits well with the conclusion of Eagly and Steffen (1984, 1986) that it is not the capabilities of men and women that inform us most powerfully, but instead it is the distribution of men and women in roles that informs our inferences.

Subjects in Sapiro's and Leeper's experiments were not fickle toward female candidates because they thought the female unfit (in fact, they were equally supportive of women). However, the subjects' understanding of the distribution of gender roles and political office led them to conclude that a female victory was less likely than a male victory. The power of the distribution argument is also attractive given the fact that in both experiments male and female subjects responded with largely the same reactions to the gender manipulations. If the beliefs about female candidates were based simply on an outgroup bias, for example, one would expect that female subjects would produce very different responses than male subjects.

Gitelson and Gitelson (1981) found that students' reactions to hypothetical male and female candidates were made very similar by providing the additional information of who won the race. When male winners and female winners were compared, their personality, effort, and likely future were judged to be quite similar. Providing just the gender of the candidates and not the outcome, however, produced assumptions of a greater likelihood of victory for the man. This again suggests the distribution effect, since there was no prejudice after the subjects were told who won. In this case, the role information overwhelms the gender influence.

The assumption of male leadership superiority in real-world situations has also been shown to wane with contact with a successful female in a new role. Ferber, Huber, and Spitze (1979) found that those who had contact with at least one female professional were more likely to accept further contact with female professionals and to rate their experience with female professionals highly. Meanwhile, in an analogous finding, MacManus (1981) studied reactions to female candidates in Houston after the city elected its first female city leader. MacManus found that people were more supportive of female candidates after they had experienced one female in office. Moreover, she found that those who paid more attention to politics were more affected by the election of the first woman. This suggests that those who were aware of the new woman and her performance were most influenced by it. Both these cases support the distribution effect, where initial uncomfortability due to a lack of prevalence was overcome by contact with a new gender-occupation relationship (a female professional or a female politician)--in other words, a new distribution. This contrasts dramatically with the outgroup effect, where amount of contact does not influence behavior or evaluation (Jones, Wood, and Quattrone 1981; Eagly and Wood 1982).

Interestingly, while there is controversy on whether prospective women candidates are subject to party bias, there is a strong consensus that once women become incumbents they are treated as well as male incumbents by the party (Burrell 1990; Werner 1993; McLean 1994). This is perhaps the strongest real-world evidence of the distribution effect. If party leaders were biased against women based on an outgroup effect, the bias should persist regardless of whether a woman is running for office or has won an office. The distribution effect, on the other hand, would suggest that party leaders could adjust their assessment of an officeholding woman based on a change in the distribution of officeholders and the acquisition of greater role information.

Just as in professional golf, where players are automatically invited to compete in tournaments after they have won a major event, candidates' worth is assumed after they have established they can win. In both endeavors, before the initial win there is a scramble to establish oneself that stymies countless competitors. While this pattern may be illuminating with regard to the distribution effect, it is also significant in explaining why many scholars could have concluded that there was no party bias against women. Studies that confined themselves to examining the treatment of winners (e.g., McLean 1994) were seeing an entirely different process (where worth was assumed and gender faded from importance) than that faced by those competing to establish themselves (where ambiguous information and external validation may hurt a disproportionate share of women).

Another example of what appears to be the distribution effect appeared in Pritchard's (1992) study of races in the Florida state legislature. Pritchard found that in years in which the state house had undergone major redistricting, female candidates were significantly more likely to be recruited to run. Clearly, women candidates are just as much in the outgroup in a redistricting year as in other years. On the other hand, a party leader's understanding of the traits and tendencies of the electorate is greatly changed in a redistricting year, as towns (and their resident interests) are shifted between districts. In these redistricting years, the party leader's sense of the distribution of traits necessary to win is weakened, and their belief that female candidates will not win presumably fades.

In a case study of a politically centered environmental group, Cable (1992) documents that the division of labor within the political group reflected the distribution of roles in home and work settings. The women were excluded from the group's strategic and public tasks and were left to play a supporting role. This arrangement lasted until the group clearly needed some of its women members to take a more active role in the group's central tasks. As need grew, the division of labor that had once subjugated the talents of women faded away without protest. The women who assumed more active roles were just as successful as the men in their efforts for the group. This example suggests that distribution-based beliefs can have an important effect on the division of labor in a political group, but since the distribution based beliefs are not motivated by animosity or perceived distance, changing circumstances can alter the beliefs and the behaviors they produce.

Studies of political activity by Gugin (1986) and Miller (1986) also point toward a distribution effect. Both Gugin and Miller find that, in the United States, political elites value experience in top-level decision-making positions in large organizations--which in practical terms translates to those with experience in the business world. This choice of test favors men, not because they are inherently more talented, but because men tend to occupy the positions that are most valued. In comparison, Gugin finds that women have an easier time gaining acceptance entering British politics, not because the British value women more, but because the British do not place as much emphasis on the types of experiences women are less likely to have. Seligman and colleagues (1974) and Matthews (1984) emphasize that, as a shortcut, recruiters tend to look for new candidates in the same places they previously had found candidates. Even for the lowest levels of political office, new candidates are sought in settings likely to be populated by males (Binning, Blumberg, and Green 1995). If women did not hold the jobs or participate in the activities that previous candidates had, then the distribution of women would be disadvantageous to their political advancement. In sum, according to the logic of the distribution effect, women have difficulty gaining the confidence of political leaders because they do not resemble the average officeholder, nor do they tend to hold the types of positions from which valued prospective officeholders are courted.

The discussion of the outgroup and distribution effects shows that there is evidence supporting the existence of both forms of bias. These examples are, however, interpretations of studies that were not conceived to directly test for the prevalence of the two forms of bias. Instead, these examples are merely suggestive that either form could exist and play an important role in politics. What is needed to draw a more firm conclusion is a study that directly tests for the two sources of bias. Perhaps the most important distinction between the outgroup and distribution explanations is that the distribution effect suggests that by altering the number of women in high-status positions, opposition to women will wane, making it easier for women in the future to pursue political office (Eagly, Makhijani, and Klonsky 1992). As Yount (1986) explains it, the division of labor feeds gender beliefs, and those beliefs help sustain the division of labor. If women can overcome the obstacles in their path to contest and win political office, the distribution will change, changing the beliefs and encouraging further change in the distribution. The outgroup effect, conversely, produces bias against those from other groups even as the other group strengthens itself politically (Giles and Evans 1985), as the talents of the outgroup may be downplayed in ego-protective conclusions (Snyder and Miene 1994). Finally, the need for further study in this area is emphasized by that fact that a comprehensive review of psychological literature on the evaluation of women in leadership roles produced inconclusive results with regard to the types, prevalence, and situational variations of bias against women (Eagly, Makhijani, and Klonsky 1992).

RESEARCH DESIGN

Why are there so few women serving in state legislatures? Theories can be sorted into supply-based explanations, which focus on the traits of women who could run for office, and demand-based explanations, which focus on the behavior of those who influence electoral events. The supply-based explanations are insufficient because women have increasingly attained the skills and interests necessary for office and show no deficiency that prevents them from pursuing office. Of the important actors in the demand equation, voter and contributor bias are not attractive explanations because of the great many studies that have failed to demonstrate such bias against women candidates. Thus, consideration of a substantial array of explanations has led to the behavior of party recruiters and the decision making of potential women candidates as the critical step in the women's officeholding equation. Here, the demand for women candidates is communicated by party leaders and interpreted by potential women candidates, and could result in prejudiced party leaders systematically limiting the number of women pursuing office.

From this conception of the process, two central questions emerge: How much bias exists? and What motivates biased behavior? This study will address these questions in three steps. First, an examination of the prevalence of the two hypothesized forms of perceptual bias will be presented. Second, the correlates or determinants of each form of bias will be considered. Third, the effects of bias on women's legislative candidacies will be investigated.

To begin designing a test for these central questions requires ruling out impractical ideas. Ideally, one would simply ask party leaders if they discriminate against women and why they would do such a thing. Unfortunately, not only would it be unlikely that any party leader would answer such a question, but some research suggests that they would be incapable of revealing their true motivations (Jackman and Muha 1984). One could base a study simply on the number of women recruited by party leaders. Unfortunately, this introduces the problem that some party leaders may know fewer women for reasons beyond prejudice, such as the level of activity of women's groups in the area or the number of women volunteers in the party. To avoid uncontrollable differences in the real world, one could take a sample of members of the party elite and subject them to a rigorous experiment in which they would be forced to choose between men and women candidates, with all other outside influences controlled. It would be impractical, however, to try to bring party leaders into a laboratory for study. Another possible alternative would be to have student subjects simulate the role of party leaders. The value of this approach is limited since the distribution and outgroup effects have already been demonstrated in the laboratory, and repeating that with simulated party leaders will bring us no closer to knowing whether actual party leaders engage in these types of behavior.

The best remaining approach to address the interaction between party leaders and potential women candidates is to survey both groups. Party leaders will be asked their attitudes toward women candidates, with the questions being sensitive to the likely need for the party leader to avoid appearing prejudiced. Potential women candidates will be asked both about their experiences with party leaders and their likely future in politics. Surveys offer the chance that both groups will participate and will provide at least correlational evidence on the existence of elite bias against women. The obvious weakness of a survey effort is the inability to control for every influence that might affect the elites' behavior and the candidates' decisions and, by extension, the results.

THE SAMPLE

The sample population for such surveys includes party elites and potential women legislative candidates from the states of Ohio, New Jersey, Tennessee, and California. Sampling four states provides regional balance as well as variation of state political cultures, attitudes toward women, and state legislative structures. As Table 3.1 reveals, these four states do represent a wide range of conditions on such relevant measures as number of elected women, attitudes toward women, state legislative pay, and party strength. While obviously not as powerful as a sample population of all 50 states, one could argue that results found to be consistent in these four varied states would be quite instructive regarding the situation in the nation as a whole. Limiting the sample to four states also allows for the addition of complementary contextual data, such as election results and demographics, which would be quite difficult to gather on the national level.

As a sample of the party elite, county party chairs will be surveyed. County party chairs serve as an excellent sample population of party elites because they have been previously identified as being very important figures in local politics in general (Pomper 1965) and in the recruitment of state legislative candidates specifically (Frendreis et al. 1994; Frendreis, Gibson, and Vertz 1990). The overwhelming majority of county party chairs, in fact, report activity in state legislative recruiting (Gibson, Frendreis, and Vertz 1989). In addition, party chairs are not too hard to find given that they typically have offices in county seats, and they are not so important that they are likely to ignore all survey requests (Gibson, Frendreis, and Vertz 1989). Legislative district lines also frequently conform to county boundaries (Aistrup 1993). Adding to the appeal of the county party chair sample is the finding that, regardless of their specific position, elites involved in the electoral process tend to be a very homogeneous group (Moscow 1948; Patterson and Boynton 1970; Baer and Bositis 1988; Montjoy, Shaffer, and Weber 1980). That is, regardless of whether one is a party chair, a party leader with a different title, or an unofficial participant, researchers have found a similarity of background and attitude that suggests a sample of county party chairs would be quite informative regarding the larger population of involved elites (Moscow 1948; Patterson and Boynton 1970; Baer and Bositis 1988; Montjoy, Shaffer, and Weber 1980). Together, these findings support the notion that party chairs are a useful group to sample because they are likely to be involved in the recruiting process and to be very much like other elite participants in terms of background, attitudes, and behavior.

The survey of party chairs is complemented with a survey of a sample of women holding local office in the four states. Those elected on the local level represent the most fertile ground for finding state legislative candidates (Hogan 1995; Carroll 1994); thus locally elected women would be able to express the perceptions of potential female state legislative candidates. This unconventional sample avoids the widespread problem of surveys relying on state legislators, a sample that constricts variation on a key dimension-success of legislative candidacy. The women in this sample are only potential legislative candidates, a

Table 3.1
Comparison of the Four States in 1995

	California	New Jersey	Ohio	Tennessee
Region[a]	West	Middle Atlantic	Midwest	South
Number of Elected Women (in thirds)[b]	1	2	1	3
Attitudes toward Women (in thirds)[c]	1	2	2	3
Political Culture[d]	Moralistic	Individualistic	Individualistic	Traditionalistic
State Legislative Pay[b]	$52,500	$35,000	$42,400	$16,000
Population Per County[b]	512,000	366,000	123,000	50,500
State House Party Margin[b]	even	Republicans control 65%	Republicans control 56%	Democrats control 59%
Party Organization Strength[e]	R-moderately strong D-moderately strong	R-strong D-strong	R-strong D-moderately weak	D-weak R-moderately strong

[a]*Source*: census designation.
[b]*Source*: Duncan and Lawrence (1995).
[c]*Source*: Werner (1993). The lowest score represents the states with the most friendly attitudes toward women's participation.
[d]*Source*: Elazar (1984).
[e]*Source*: Cotter et al. (1984) except for New Jersey, which is based on my application of the Cotter et al. work.

group that includes both those who have been encouraged and discouraged from seeking higher office, making the group uniquely qualified to express the extent and ramifications of bias. Moreover, direct combatants in political contests can be overwhelmed by the outcome of the contest and lose the ability to distinguish their honest perceptions of the political world from their outcome-based beliefs (Kingdon 1966). Again, a reliance on potential candidates rather than actual candidates may yield more accurate responses. By comparing their responses with those of party chairs, a more instructive look at the interaction between these groups will develop, far more instructive than would be possible by surveying only party chairs or only locally elected women.

County Party Chair Survey

Each county chair was mailed a survey asking questions on their job, opinions, and recruitment practices. A total of 516 county party chairs actively held office in the four states in the fall of 1995. Names and addresses of the county party chairs were provided by the state party offices of the two parties in each state.

Party chairs were asked a series of questions requesting that they offer their evaluation of candidates with certain traits (e.g., occupation, personality, gender). The existence of the distribution effect will be assessed by comparing the relationship between the prevalence of traits and the evaluation offered by the party chairs. More specifically, if the distribution effect is influencing party chair perceptions, then their reaction to candidate traits (such as occupation, personality, and gender) should be governed by the distribution of these traits in politics. The more typical or the higher the distribution of the trait, the more positive reaction it should elicit. Meanwhile, the existence of the outgroup effect will be assessed by comparing the relationship between similarity and evaluation. If the outgroup effect is influencing party chairs, they should not react to the prevalence of the candidate trait, but instead they should react positively to traits more closely associated with themselves. Here, for example, male party chairs should react more favorably to traits associated with men.

In addition to measures designed to assess types of bias, other questions are necessary to assess the origins and influence of bias. Among the determinants of perceptual bias that have been found in previous research are time pressure, power over outcomes, accountability, outcome dependency, rigidity, and exposure to diverse experiences. Party chairs are asked how they do their job (e.g., how they recruit, how often they recruit), how confident they are in their work (e.g., confidence in assessments of candidates), the situation they work in (e.g., party strength, ideology of district), and about their personal background (e.g., age, education, occupation, family influence) in an effort to create measures related to the factors found in previous research. The relationship between each of the measures and the party chairs' amount of outgroup or distribution bias will then be assessed. Most basically, this will provide the correlates of bias. These results can also be used to link those correlates with the previously established theories in order to shed light on the success of those theories in explaining party chair attitudes.

After addressing the amount of bias and the determinants of bias, the third major component of this research will be addressing the effect of bias on women's candidacies for the state legislature. By incorporating variables found to be significant in other studies, such as women's party activity, party strength, and political culture, the import of bias as a determinant of women's candidacies will be assessed. Beyond limiting the number of women who run, another possibility that will be investigated is that biased party chairs encourage women to run in longshot races, which will be assessed by incorporating a measure of the competitiveness of the districts.

Potential Women Candidate Survey

The survey of women candidates will be relied on to build a foundation for the argument that women potential candidates are subject to biased treatment, to shed light on whether bias retards all women candidates or just some types of women candidates, and to offer comparative information on matters such as women's party activity (to provide an assessment independent of party chairs). A sample of elected women was chosen to produce 516 cases, the same number available for party chairs. The sample consisted of 129 women randomly chosen from the lists available for each of the four states. Names and addresses of locally elected women in the four states were provided by the National League of Cities.

The sample of elected women was surveyed in a similar fashion to the county party chairs. Potential women candidates were asked about their perceptions and experiences with bias in the political system. These responses provide primary evidence to help establish a foundation for the argument that women face bias. Their reports also allow us to better understand the mechanisms through which bias affects potential women candidates.

Potential women candidates were asked to express their interest in running for office given different scenarios and were also asked a series of questions concerning such matters as their ideology, issue positions, and personality traits. In addition to indicating how many women are affected by biased party chairs, this information will offer unique evidence in establishing the ultimate ramifications of bias. If women who are most likely to overcome elite bias and discouragement have different characteristics than the women who will by stopped by bias, this suggests another significant result of bias in the form of a limitation not just on the number of women who proceed but also on the types of women who proceed.

Finally, potential women candidates were also asked a battery of questions patterned on the party chair survey items. By offering assessments on such matters as women's interest and activity in politics, responses to questions with obvious self-serving or socially desirable implications for the party chairs can be compared with the independently provided women's responses. Such comparisons will allow adjustments to be made in cases where the party chairs appear to give self-serving responses. In the process, confidence in the final results will be strengthened.

T-tests, correlations, and regression analyses of the relationships that appear will be used to attempt to assess the prevalence of the two types of bias, their causes, and their ramifications on potential women candidates. These three steps--establishing the types of bias, establishing their determinants, and establishing the effects of bias--will be addressed individually in three chapters. More detail on the applicable research design is provided in each chapter.

SURVEY DESIGN AND MAILING

The survey instruments for both the county chairs and the potential women candidates were designed following Dilman's (1978) procedures for mail surveys. Both surveys were sent in the form of an 8.5" x 5.5"-size booklet consisting of eight pages of questions. Each survey was accompanied by a cover letter and postage paid return envelope (see Appendix A and Appendix B for the cover letters and surveys). All material carried the Ohio State University logo. The cover letters for both groups stated that their individual response was quite important as they were part of a limited sample, who provided their name and address, and an assurance that their names would never be used in analyzing or reporting the results.

In order to minimize the inclination to offer socially desirable responses or to respond to demand characteristics, the cover letter also stated that this was a study of the candidate/party leader relationship, not specifically mentioning gender. Most of the questions did not have explicit gender implications. Also, throughout the survey instrument, emphasis was placed on the idea that expert opinions were being sought and that there were no right or wrong answers. This was an attempt to remind respondents that their political assessments were not necessarily their political preferences, again in an effort to reduce respondents' inclination to feel responsible for the implications of each response.

The surveys were mailed in order to arrive in the days immediately following Election Day, November 1995. This date was chosen to allow local election work to have been completed and to allow time for responses before holidays and winter vacations inhibited county chairs and potential women candidates from responding.

One week after the surveys were mailed, a follow-up postcard was sent to everyone in the two samples. The postcards simply reminded the recipients that a survey had been sent to them and asked that they complete it at their earliest convenience.

Response Rate

A total of 280 usable surveys were returned by the county party chairs, a response rate of 54%. The potential women candidates returned 276 surveys, a

Table 3.2
Comparison of Full Sample to Respondents

Party Chairs

Party	% of Sample	% of Respondents
Democrats	50	49
Republicans	50	51
State		
CA	22	20
NJ	8	8
OH	35	39
TN	35	33

Women Candidates

Office Held	% of Sample	% of Respondents
City Council	80	82
Mayor	15	14
Other	5	4
State		
CA	25	23
NJ	25	24
OH	25	27
TN	25	26

response rate of 53%. While such response rates are not ideal, they are consistent with the typical rates achieved with elite samples (Frendreis, Gibson, and Vertz 1990). More importantly, a comparison of the full sample with the respondents reveals that the county party chairs and potential women candidates who returned the surveys quite closely resemble the full samples. There are no statistically significant differences (at the $p < .10$) in the demographic characteristics presented in Table 3.2. Establishing the respondents and the overall sample to be similar offers some indication that the patterns that emerge in the data are not likely aberrations caused by a select responding group.

SUMMARY

The two explanations of elite bias, the distribution and outgroup effects, need to be explored because the ramifications of the two processes differ greatly. More optimistically, the distribution theory suggests that, merely by increasing the number of elected women or improving women's standing in professional careers, elites will react by increasing their acceptance and enthusiasm for female candidacies because their understanding of the distribution of roles will cl

The outgroup effect, more ominously, would predict that male party elites will remain reluctant to support female candidacies regardless of any improvement in the distribution of women in work or in politics.

After addressing the prevalence of these forms of perceptual bias, this research will explore the determinants of bias. Certainly, if these forms of bias are found, it is important to know where we are most likely and least likely to find them. This will tell us not only where we might expect to find women candidates in the future, but also what we might do to discourage bias in the present. The third and final component of this effort is the question of the effect of these forms of bias. How important are these theories of perceptual bias in explaining the lack of women legislators?   Do these theories help explain patterns that were unaccounted for in previous research?

The study of women's candidacies has suffered from a dearth of direct analysis of the participants' attitudes and behaviors, and this design aims to correct for those deficiencies. Regardless of which bias provides a stronger explanation, what its correlates are, or what estimated effects emerge, what is apparent is that the thought patterns and interactions between elite party recruiters and potential women candidates represent a most promising frontier from which to explore the paucity of women legislators.

4

The Shape of Bias

As has been argued in previous chapters, the role of party elites in the process of electing women has often been ignored. When party elites have been studied, frequently their role has been surmised from indirect evidence instead of more direct examination of their attitudes and behaviors. This occurs despite the fact that there is ample evidence that party elites have an important part in candidate decision making, and that there is reason to suspect such elites might display bias against women. Two promising explanations, the distribution effect and the outgroup effect, have been offered as potential forms of bias against women candidates.

This chapter will first utilize the survey of potential women candidates to see if they report experiences consistent with party elite bias. Then, party chair responses will be scrutinized to see if their expressed candidate preferences betray indications of the outgroup effect or the distribution effect.

BIAS AGAINST WOMEN

Women holding local office serve here as a sample of potential women candidates for the state legislature. Local officeholders represent a wide range of experiences and amounts of success, likely including those who will one day serve in the state legislature and those who will be stopped along the way. These potential candidates for the state legislature were asked, "In your experience, have party leaders discouraged potential women candidates from running for office because of their gender?" A stunning 64% responded affirmatively. Space was provided for the respondents to make comments on the question, and 46% of the women chose to relate some personal experience with discrimination. While it is hard to deny the disquieting nature of the purely statistical frequency of gender bias reported by these women, it is even harder to ignore the problem when they individually recount their experiences in their own words.

Merely examining a handful of the comments provides a useful foundation in combating the notion that women do not face bias at the hands of political elites and political parties. Figure 4.1 presents the prevalence of various occurrences of bias among those who reported experiencing discrimination. Many responses referred to some variant of "old-boy networks," where appointments, endorsements, and eventually nominations went to male friends of the men in charge instead of going to the person most qualified. Others recounted situations in which they were discouraged from running because of their gender or were ignored or rebuffed when they attempted to assume leadership on a specific issue.

Through the course of their political experiences, these women report being told in various ways that when it came to running for office, they "Don't belong here. You should be at home in your kitchen,"[1] that the job of holding office "really needs a man."[2] To the extent their political activity was accepted, it was accepted with severe limits, as one Ohio Republican reports being told that in her party, "Women only serve on the decorating and coffee committee." Nevertheless, these women continued to persevere, enduring insults along the way, including being "Referred to as a Dumb Housewife,"[3] a "blonde bimbo,"[4] or "brainless bitches,"[5] being told they "spend money like a woman,"[6] or that holding office made women "frighteningly strong to their husbands."[7] More startlingly, some women referred to even more pervasive bias, that affected everything they did politically. In the words of one Ohio Democrat, the instances of discrimination she experienced in party politics were "Too numerous to list, I could write a book!"

How can one reconcile the reports of bias these women offer with the popular scholarly conclusion that women are not discriminated against by party leaders? The comments of one California Democrat are quite instructive on this question: "Women in the party are to rise no higher than volunteer work. Women elected to office rarely come from the party, but run from the outside. If they win, the party quickly embraces them." In other words, just as was previously argued, if one examined the party's behavior with regard to officeholders and nominees, one would find no bias. It is only when one searches deeper and examines the treatment of potential candidates that the efforts to slow women are apparent.

Establishing that women are subject to bias within their party is a significant step in justifying a need to examine party recruiter behavior and the larger effort to identify bias. These simple data strongly suggest that potential women candidates are subject to bias.

Objections, however, could be raised to this finding. Notably, experience with discrimination might have encouraged women to complete the survey; thus the result may reflect this tendency rather than the true amount of bias. There are a couple of useful responses to this objection. First, as Table 4.1 illustrates, reporting party bias was not correlated with the woman's ideology, her year of birth, her level of education, the ideology of the voters, or her party (no relationship significant at $p < .10$). In other words, rather than discrimination reports emerging from a select

Figure 4.1
Types of Discriminatory Treatment Reported

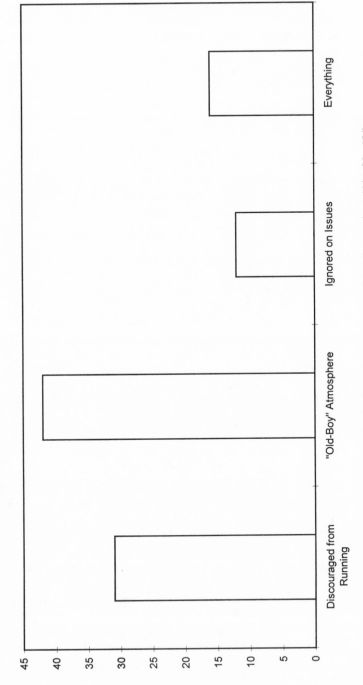

Note : Column sizes refer to relative percentages reporting that form of treatment among those who experienced bias (N = 174).

Table 4.1
Correlates of Discrimination in Recruitment Reported by Women Candidates

Ideology of Woman Candidate	-.09[a]
Age of Woman Candidate	.04
Education of Woman Candidate	.04
Party of Woman Candidate	.07
Ideology of Voters	.11

N = 275.

[a]Coding: Ideology seven-point scale (1 = Very Liberal, 7 = Very Conservative); Age last two digits of year of birth; education five-point scale (1 = less than high school, 5 = advanced degree); party (1 = Democrat, 2 = Republican).

Note: None of the relationships reach statistical significance at p < .10.

group of women with rare features, discrimination was felt by a great diversity of women, suggesting a pervasiveness of bias. Second, the question on bias was in the second half of the survey. That coupled with the many respondents who took the time to comment that they had not experienced bias suggests experience with bias was not a major factor in deciding whether to return the survey. Finally, while the women respondents are potential candidates for the state legislature, they all have been elected on the local level. Thus, before their reports are dismissed as the insignificant carping of conspiracists, it should be remembered that these are people who have experienced some success in politics, and therefore their encounters with bias should be treated quite seriously.

OUTGROUP VERSUS DISTRIBUTION EFFECT

If there is significant bias, as this and some other research suggest (Werner 1993), what motivates such bias? Why would party leaders exhibit a preference for male candidates over female candidates? Are party chairs more likely to favor male candidates because of an outgroup effect, or is the distribution effect influencing party chair behavior?

The fundamental difference between the outgroup and distribution effects is simply the origin of negative presumptions. The outgroup effect posits that assumptions of similar beliefs and positive initial evaluations are fostered by surface similarity with the evaluator, while those who are outwardly dissimilar are treated as members of a homogenous and less esteemed group. The distribution effect, on the other hand, does not hinge on estimates of similarity with the evaluator. Instead, the distribution effect is derived from essentially statistical conclusions that certain types of people (i.e., men) are more likely to hold high-status positions. For the purposes of this study, the question becomes: Are women devalued politically because they are outgroup members to male chairs, or are they devalued because there are few women in high-status positions such as public office?

These effects can be explored by examining the evaluation of traits to see whether prevalence or similarity leads to a more positive reaction. There are two central tests that suggest themselves in this situation. First, do party chairs respond to the distribution of traits? The distribution effect predicts evaluations will be based on observed distributions such as the occupational background or gender of officeholders. The outgroup effect, on the other hand, should produce no reaction to the prevalence of an occupation or to the number of women in office. This can be operationalized by comparing the reactions of party chairs in situations where there is a known distribution of a trait.

Second, do party chair evaluations vary by the gender of the chair? Both male and female party chairs see a world where fewer officeholders are women. If the distribution effect is influencing their behavior, both male and female party chairs should express severe reservations about the prospects of female candidates. Conversely, if party chairs are influenced by the outgroup effect, the behavior of male and female party chairs should vary dramatically as male party chairs (who make up 85% of the sample) react negatively toward potential women candidates, but female party chairs (for whom women candidates are not in an outgroup) react much more positively toward potential women candidates. This is simply operationalized by comparing male party chairs' and female party chairs' reaction to the same genderized stimulus.

The responses of county party chairs to the survey instrument will be utilized to assess their attitudes. Built into the survey were numerous opportunities for party chairs to evaluate relevant candidate traits. The evaluations involved reactions to occupations, reactions to personality traits, estimates of women's electoral chances in specific scenarios and over time, and finally, reports on the gender ratio of the candidates the chairs consider most capable of seeking state legislative office.

Occupation Test

In the first evaluation, the party chairs were asked to rate the favorability of candidates with different occupations. Specifically, the chairs, being told only the occupation of the candidates, were asked to rank each of the seven candidates based on their capacity to win a race for the state legislature (on a scale of 1-7, 7 = most desirable). The occupations listed were attorney, grade school teacher, television reporter, sales person, former professional athlete, police officer, and "someone with your primary occupation." If the distribution effect influences the party chairs, then they should rate most favorably the occupations that tend to produce elected officials. In order to facilitate such a comparison, Figure 4.2 depicts the proportion of legislative candidates in 1994 from the occupational

Figure 4.2
Occupational Background of Legislative Candidates

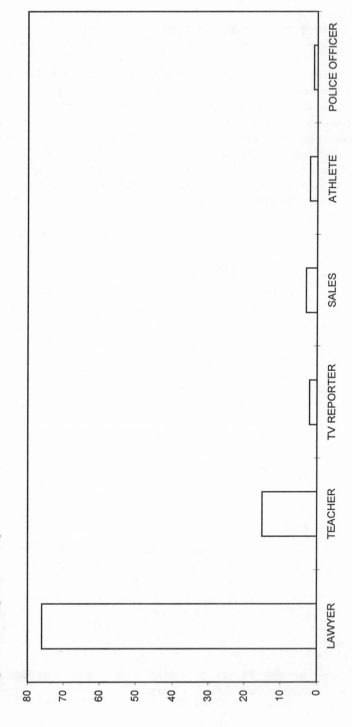

Note: Column sizes refer to relative percentages of legislative candidates among the occupations listed.

Table 4.2
Party Chair Rating of Candidates from Different Occupations

Attorney	4.3[a]
Grade School Teacher	4.2
Television Reporter	3.4
Sales	4.3
Former Professional Athlete	3.5
Police Officer	3.7
Someone with your Primary Occupation	5.5

N = 280.

[a]Scores represent the average response to a seven-point ranking scale (1 = least favorable, 7 = most favorable).

backgrounds listed.   If the outgroup effect influences party chairs, then chairs should rate most favorably the occupations that are most closely related to their own background.

As Table 4.2 illustrates, party chairs did not display a strong preference for the occupations that have the strongest presence, or distribution, in politics. While attorneys play the most significant role by far in legislative officeholding of the professions listed, attorney was not the top-rated category, and certainly did not stand far ahead of the field as its distribution in politics would suggest. The overall correlation between the occupation ratings and their distribution was weak ($r = .17$) and statistically insignificant (at $p < .10$). Conversely, strong evidence for the outgroup effect exists as the clear top choice of party chairs was a candidate from the same profession as themselves.

This evidence could be misleading if responses to a candidate from the same profession as the chair vary based on the type or distribution of that profession. To examine this possibility, party chairs were also asked to list their primary occupation. Table 4.3 reveals that party chair reaction was quite favorable across all occupation categories. Management, educators, advanced degree professionals, farmers and laborers, and clerical and support workers all produced favorable responses from party chairs with these backgrounds. In fact, examining the responses on an individual level shows that party chairs from such diverse callings as cosmetologist, architect, and union shop steward all chose to rate their profession as the most desirable of the seven listed. In other words, party chairs did not respond to their own occupation based on its prevalence in politics but instead seemed to respond favorably based merely on its familiarity in their own lives.

Table 4.3
Party Chair Rating of Candidates from Own "Primary Occupation" by Type of Occupation

Clerical/Support Staff	5.6[a]
Farmer/Laborer	5.5
Education	5.7
Managerial	5.4
Professional (Advanced Degree)	5.5

N = 260.

[a]Scores represent the average response to a seven-point ranking scale (1 = least favorable, 7 = most favorable).

Further evidence for an outgroup effect is gleaned when responses to the occupation categories are divided based on party chair gender. Specifically, when examining the two occupations most likely to be associated with a specific gender, grade school teacher with women and professional athlete with men, it appears that the reaction to candidates from these two professions is strongly influenced by the gender of the party chair. Female party chairs react far more positively to the grade school teacher than do male party chairs (male chairs = 4.0/female chairs = 4.7, difference significant at $p < .05$),[8] and male party chairs react far more positively to the professional athlete than do female chairs (male chairs = 3.7/female chairs = 2.8, difference significant at $p < .01$). In sum, both men and women appear to react more favorably to those candidates they would expect to be in their ingroup than they react to candidates assumed to be in their outgroup.

It is both a strength and a weakness of this type of test that gender was not specifically mentioned to the respondents. The strength of this measure is that it is less likely to provoke defensive responses used to guard against the appearance of gender bias. The weakness, however, is that such efforts make it more difficult to show that respondents would react this way when gender was the clear focus of their attention. To extend these findings and move closer to the target, party chairs were asked to react to a series of personality traits. This is another effort to examine how party chairs feel about male and female candidates without that purpose being explicitly apparent.

Personality Trait Test

The party chairs were given a list of 15 personality traits and were asked whether the trait was a positive or negative feature of a candidate for the state legislature. Then the party chairs were asked to rate the importance of the trait to electoral success on a scale from 1 (least important) to 7 (most important). The trait list was constructed to provide five traits typically associated with men, five typically associated with women, and five with no gender association. To make the purpose of the test less obvious, the traits were randomly listed in the survey question.

For each trait, positive responses were scored as 1, negative responses as -1. This number was multiplied by the importance rating, resulting in an ultimate possible range of -7 (negative, highest importance) to 7 (positive, highest importance) for any trait. From these scores, a female trait index and a male trait index were created by taking the average of the five scores for the traits in each category. The potential range for the five-trait female or male index would therefore be -7 to 7. The more positive and important the traits were judged to be, the higher the resulting score. Negative, important traits obviously most dramatically reduced the score.

Similarly, the neutral traits were used to examine the response to prevalent and less prevalent traits. The average response to the two most prevalent traits can be compared to the average response to the three less prevalent traits on the same -7 to 7 range.

First, the correlation between evaluation of female traits and the distribution of female officeholders will be calculated. Second, the relationship between the prevalence of traits and their importance rating will be examined. Third, comparison will be made between the responses of male and female party chairs within each index. As was argued earlier, if the distribution effect is coloring party chair responses, positive evaluations should flow from higher distributions, and there should be no significant difference between the responses of men and women because both groups are observing the same distribution in politics. The outgroup effect, on the other hand, should reveal no positive effect of distribution and should result in both genders increasing the importance of their ingroup's traits while devaluing the importance of their outgroup's traits.

The results provide strong support for the outgroup effect. First, there is a slight negative association between distribution of female officeholders and ratings of female traits ($r = -.11$). A correlation that is neither statistically significant nor positive is quite inconsistent with the distribution effect. Second, party chairs did not rate the traits that are most prevalent in politics more favorably. Party chairs rated the two least prevalent traits (average score 5.2) to be the two most positive/important of the five neutral traits (the less prevalent traits averaged 2.1). Again, the party chairs failed to treat that which is more commonly associated with officeholders as superior, challenging the distribution effect. Finally, male party chairs rate the male traits much higher than do the female party chairs. Male party chairs offer estimates of male trait value that are higher by a margin representing fully 10% of the range of the trait index (Male Trait Index: male chairs = 3.1/female chairs = 1.7, $p < .01$). Meanwhile, female chairs, by an even wider margin, rate the female traits higher than do male party chairs (Female Trait Index: male chairs = 1.9/female chairs = 3.4, $p < .01$). Again, such a pattern should not occur if chairs are influenced by the distribution effect, but this is precisely the pattern one would expect if the outgroup effect is influencing perceptions.

On two measures, the occupation ranking and the personality trait response, the party chairs have displayed strong support for the outgroup effect by favoring that which is more closely associated with themselves and devaluing descriptions of outgroup members. Their responses have lent no support to the distribution effect as prevalence has not produced more positive evaluations. Although the results to this point have been clear, gender has not been explicitly mentioned to the respondents. Therefore, one could argue that a stronger test of the applicability of the outgroup and distribution effects on gender bias would require the party chairs to respond more directly to gender (Linville and Jones 1980).

Electoral Chances of Women

The next evaluation, then, explicitly asks for estimates of the electoral chances of women. Specifically, the first set of questions will center on the party chairs' opinions of a woman's chances for election to a set of political offices. The list progresses from local offices to national offices, including town/city council, state house, and Congress. The party chairs were asked to indicate on a scale of 0 to 100 the likelihood of a female candidate from their party defeating a male for the position in the general election (0 = no chance, 100 = certain victory). The scenario varied from incumbent to challenger, and candidates emphasizing "mainstream issues" to candidates emphasizing "women's issues."[9] In order to lessen the chance for self-monitoring (avoiding giving an answer that reflects poorly on yourself), the survey emphasized that the question asks for a guess based on their experience and expertise, and not who they would prefer. In this way, the subjects should not feel that they are betraying any bias when they are rating the chances for victory of the hypothetical female.

In the aggregate, if women and men party chairs are similarly skeptical of the chances of women candidates, and a higher distribution in the real world produces more positive ratings, this would clearly offer support for a distribution effect since the responses would not be predicated on ingroup/outgroup status but would instead reflect the prevalence of women in politics. Conversely, if the distribution does not affect ratings and if male party chairs are more negative toward women, this suggests an outgroup effect.

In addition to examining the aggregate response to these scenarios, responses to specific situations are also of interest. The level of office was varied because as the offices rise in prestige, women are less likely to hold them. The rate of women officeholders is much higher on the local level than on the state level, and much higher at the state level than in Congress (Carroll 1994). According to the saliency of the numerically rare aspect of the distribution effect (Eagly, Makhijani, and Klonsky 1992), party chairs should therefore express more skepticism about the chances of women at higher levels of office. If party chairs judge women to be less likely to win at the highest levels, this would suggest the distribution effect. The outgroup explanation, on the other hand, implies a general preference for male

Table 4.4
Party Chairs' Estimated Electoral Chances of Women Candidates by Situation

Status	Chance of Success[a]
Incumbent	54
Challenger	45*

Level of Office	Chance of Success
Local	54
State	49
National	45*

N = 274.

*difference significant at p < .05
[a]on a scale from 0 to 100 (0 = no chance, 100 = certain victory)

candidates even at the lowest levels. If party leaders believe women would be relatively equally unlikely to win at all three levels, this would suggest an outgroup effect.

By asking the party chairs to rate the chances of incumbents versus the chances of challengers, the leaders' attention to role information can be assessed. If they treat incumbent women's chances as they would incumbent men's, this suggests that they have used the role information over the gender information available to them, and that they are not displaying an outgroup bias (Deaux and Lewis 1984; Gitelson and Gitelson 1981). If, on the other hand, party chairs continue to downgrade the chances of an incumbent female, this strongly suggests an outgroup bias as the chairs would be ignoring the information inherent in incumbency.

With these measures, the distribution effect appears to be supported by the finding that party chairs rated women's chances for election to be lower as the level of office rose from local to state to national (Table 4.4). In other words, the distribution of officeholders appears to have influenced the response pattern in that where women's distribution is highest their chances were rated more strongly. Table 4.4 also indicates that party chairs rated women's chances as being better if they were incumbents instead of challengers, casting some doubt on the outgroup effect, as party chairs appear to attend to this individuating information. Despite these patterns, examined more broadly, the data again support the existence of an outgroup effect.

First, the aggregate women candidate electoral chance rating (average of the estimates for the 12 scenarios presented) is not strongly correlated with gender distribution of officeholders ($r = .09$). Second, the results reveal that, when averaging their responses across the different scenarios presented to them, women party chairs believe that women candidates have a significantly better chance of winning than do men party chairs (Table 4.5). This finding damages the veracity of the support for the distribution effect, as not only is a significant difference not to be expected if the distribution effect were to be creating this behavior, but the average difference between male and female party chairs is larger than the effect of level of office. Moreover, these differences between men and women party chairs exist in the same direction for all 12 situations presented (and are statistically significant in 10 of the 12).

Some might observe the results in Table 4.5 and argue that the numbers hardly bespeak great prejudice against women, as most of the figures are near 50%. However, according to male party chairs, the average chance for a woman candidate to succeed in the 12 scenarios is 47%. Clearly, 47% is less than 50%, and in a two-person race 47% is an expected loser, meaning the chair should go with another candidate. Additionally, 47% is an estimate based on half the candidacies being labeled "mainstream" on the issues. Left on their own to assume what kinds of issues women candidates would run on, party chairs might more likely imagine women running on "women's issues,"[10] for which their average estimate of the likelihood of female success ranges from a high of 47% to a low of 28%. Examining the estimates shown for "women's issue" candidates in Table 4.5 reveals that the cumulative average for such candidates offered only a 38% chance of success. In other words, 47%, which is a losing estimate, may be inflated by the "mainstream" label given to half the candidates.

While this examination of the results provides some additional support for the outgroup effect, another way to interpret the data is even more illuminating. One of the defining aspects of bias against a group is obviously the failure to attend to individuating information (Judd and Park 1988). Although party chairs did recognize the difference between incumbents and challengers, in the survey party chairs were given different scenarios involving three different levels of office, two different issue areas emphasized, and two different types of candidates. This resulted in 12 different situations in which the party chair was asked to estimate the chances of a female candidate. To the extent party chairs are without bias, they should recognize and incorporate into their estimates the value of the information provided them. In other words, beyond observing an incumbent/challenger distinction, each of the 12 estimates should vary significantly based on the precise details involved. If the distribution effect is affecting party chair behavior, this variance should not be predicted by gender of the chair. If, however, the outgroup effect is affecting party chair behavior, then male party chairs should be less likely to acknowledge the individuating information of the outgroup candidate scenarios presented and should therefore display less variance in their estimates than female party chairs display.

Table 4.5
Estimated Electoral Chances of Women Candidates by Gender of Party Chair

	Male Chairs	Female Chairs
Overall Average	47	57**
Incumbent, Mainstream, City	68	81**
Incumbent, Mainstream, State	61	71**
Incumbent, Mainstream, Congress	57	66*
Incumbent, Women, City	47	55*
Incumbent, Women, State	43	52**
Incumbent, Women, Congress	39	48*
Challenger, Mainstream, City	60	73**
Challenger, Mainstream, State	50	58*
Challenger, Mainstream, Congress	43	50
Challenger, Women, City	37	45*
Challenger, Women, State	33	40
Challenger, Women, Congress	28	36*

N = 274.

**difference significant at $p < .01$
*difference significant at $p < .05$

To examine this possibility, a score was created by calculating the variance for each individual party chair's estimates across the 12 scenarios.[11] The pattern that emerges shows that female party chairs do, in fact, have more variance in their responses to the scenarios presented them (male chairs = 369/female chairs = 499, $p < .05$). Women's estimates of women's chances vary significantly more with the details of the situation than do men's estimates. This provides further support for the outgroup effect, as women utilized the individuating details describing ingroup members more than men chose to factor in those same details when describing the chances of outgroup members.

While this test also provides support for the contention that the outgroup effect is evident in party chair behavior, all of the tests presented have relied heavily on hypothetical situations. Party chairs do not literally make decisions based on someone's occupation in isolation from everything else. Nor are party chairs likely to analyze every personality trait they encounter. While they may be more likely to encounter and evaluate a woman candidate for a particular position, they still are unlikely to have encountered women in every one of the scenarios presented to them. Therefore, the next test involves gender both directly and in a real-world setting, as party chairs are asked their opinion of women's chances over time.

As Yount (1986) and others have argued, distribution-related effects should vary over time as the distribution of roles varies. There are unquestionably more women in office today then there were 10 years ago. However, there have also been consistent analyses arguing that women's chances to win office have been equal to men's over that same time period (Darcy, Welch, and Clark 1994). Therefore, if a pattern emerges where those who see more elected women think that women's chances for election are dramatically improving, this would be evidence of the distribution effect as the estimates would not reflect women's actual chances over time but their relative distribution in politics over time. Given the objective reality that women's electoral chances have been similar to men's, if female party chairs recognize this while male party chairs perceive significant differences over time, this would be further evidence of the outgroup effect as the expression of great change among outgroup observers would likely reflect the tendency to exaggerate properties or characteristics of outgroup members (Linville and Jones 1980).[12]

To explore this in the survey, party leaders were asked: "Comparing an average female candidate for the state legislature in your state ten years ago, with an average female candidate today, how would you characterize their relative chances for victory?" A seven-point scale was provided, with 1 labeled "better chance 10 years ago," 4 labeled "same," and 7 labeled "better chance today."

An initial examination of the data yielded a somewhat surprising pattern. The overall mean response was 4.9, varying only 0.3 for male and female party chairs. This pattern displays neither the patently unrealistic perception that women's chances have improved dramatically (which would indicate the distribution effect), nor does it display a large gender gap (which might indicate an outgroup effect).

Relying on the mean response, however, hides a more interesting pattern. While women and men party chairs have similar means, the frequency distribution of their responses is quite different. Male party chairs are more likely to offer responses in the extreme categories (1, 2, 6, 7) than are the female party chairs. Female party chairs are correspondingly more likely to offer responses in the middle categories (3, 4, 5). In fact, 73% of female party chairs chose a middle category, while only 47% of male party chairs chose a middle category, a difference significant at $p < .01$. In other words, female party chairs describing ingroup candidates appear less susceptible to exaggeration than do men describing the condition of outgroup candidates. While this supports the contention that the outgroup effect is influencing party chair behavior, the distribution effect again receives no support from the relationship between prevalence and evaluation. The women's chances over time score, using the full seven-point scale, is quite weakly correlated ($r = -.05$) with the distribution of women officeholders.

With little exception, the data presented strongly support the contention that the outgroup effect influences party chair behavior, while the distribution effect has received little support. The strength of the presentation has been the consistency of the finding over situations in which gender was not explicitly a factor and situations where gender was explicitly a factor. The most significant limitation of these results is that all of the questions have relied upon hypothetical situations or estimates of attitudes. In other words, no test to this point has directly asked the party chairs about real-world behavior. This is an important limitation since there are obviously situations where attitudes measured may not result in congruent behavior (Kahn and Crosby 1987). Therefore, each test presented to this point would certainly be stronger evidence of the power of the outgroup and distribution effects if it could be linked to real-world behavior.

Gender of Future Candidates

Toward that end, in the final evaluation, party chairs were asked the gender ratio of the top five people they have in mind for future state legislative races. Party chairs were also asked the gender of the person they consider to be the best of the five. The obvious danger of this type of question is that it may appear to the party chair to be socially unacceptable to answer this question truthfully if there are too few women in their top five. A basis for optimism, however, exists in that the chairs were told this was a study of the party leader/candidate relationship (not about women) and were reminded throughout the survey that there were no right answers. If the party chairs accepted the purported purpose of the study and did not feel threatened, then they might offer realistic answers to the sensitive questions.

The distribution effect does not find support in this evaluation, either, as the number of women in the chairs' list of prospective candidates is not strongly correlated with gender distribution ($r = .12$). Further support for the outgroup effect is again apparent as male chairs indicate that 1.5 of their top five candidates are women, while women respond that 2.2 of their top five candidates are women, a difference significant at $p < .01$. Perhaps more interesting is the question of who the top candidate is, since this will presumably be the person given the most opportunity and encouragement to run. Again, whether a woman is the top choice in the chair's list of prospective candidates is not strongly correlated with gender distribution (r = .15). Moreover, while only 24% of male party chairs indicate that their top candidate for a future state legislative race is a woman, 47% of female party chairs indicate that their top candidate is a woman, a difference also significant at p < .01.

In these questions, that seek to directly tap real party chair behavior, male party chairs display a distinct pattern of more strongly supporting ingroup candidates at the expense of outgroup candidates (women). That women display no such anti-women bias, coupled with the absence of a correlation between the number of women officeholders and the presence of women on the prospective candidate list, suggests that it is not the relatively poor distribution of women in high-status positions that caused this response, but instead again this is evidence for an outgroup effect where those who lack surface similarity to the evaluator are less valued.

Moreover, as is summarized in Table 4.6, the distribution effect was not firmly supported by any of the tests utilized. The outgroup effect, however, was consistently supported by a variety of evaluations whose connection with gender ranged from none to explicit, and whose relationship with real behavior ranged from remote and hypothetical to very real.

LIMITATIONS OF THE DATA

While these findings appear strong, their limitations should be explored. Among the most relevant threats to validity in a study such as this are demand characteristics and social desirability. In short, respondents could have made up their minds as to the purpose of this research and proceeded to give answers that fit the supposed purpose. Alternatively, if they figured out that this research had to do with discrimination against women, they could have adapted their responses to conform to the socially desirable position of not being biased.

As has been mentioned, to make gender a less prominent aspect of the survey and to make these problems less of a threat, respondents were told from the outset that this was a study of the relationship between party leaders and party candidates. More importantly, as has been noted throughout, the diversity of tests used in this effort make both demand characteristics and social desirability seem unlikely. Party chairs responded consistently when gender was explicit, when it was implicit, and when it was essentially unrelated, suggesting that even when they could not have known the purpose of the question their answers were consistent with the outgroup effect. The consistent results from a diversity of tests suggest the findings are a reflection of party chair beliefs and not of the limitations of the survey instrument.

Another potential limitation for these results is the fact that male and female party chairs were not randomly assigned political beliefs or political settings. Perhaps, rather than reflecting the importance of gender (or outgroups), the

Table 4.6
Review of Major Evidence

	Distribution Effect	Outgroup Effect	Supports
Occupation	not significant	A. Favor person from own occupation B. Men more positive than women for "male" occupation; women more positive than men for "female" occupation	Outgroup
Personality	not significant	Men more positive than women for "male" traits; women more positive than men for "female" traits	Outgroup
Electoral Chances (different scenarios)	not significant	A. Men offer lower chance for women candidate than do women B. Men have less variance than women in their estimates for women candidates	Outgroup
Electoral chances (over time)	not significant	Men more extreme (more likely to exaggerate) than women on women's chances	Outgroup
Gender of Future Candidates	not significant	Male chairs have more men in the list of prospective candidates than women; male chairs more likely than women to have man as top prospective candidate	Outgroup

differences shown here between men and women party chairs reflect the different types of counties they represent or different ideologies they happen to favor. There is no perfect response to this claim, since party chairs cannot be randomly assigned beliefs or counties, and therefore all other factors cannot be made exactly equal.

However, there are two comparisons that can be made that appear to mitigate the scope of this problem. First, male and female party chairs, on average, represent quite similar counties and have similar political beliefs. As Table 4.7 illustrates, on measures of political setting, personal demographics, and the demographics of the legislative districts they operate in, male and female party chairs have no statistically significant differences (using p < .10 as benchmark). On such fundamentally important indicators of their political outlook as their ideology, the distribution of female legislators in their state, party strength, their age and race, and the income, education, and racial makeup of their districts, male and female party chairs are much more alike than they are different. This pattern is consistent with the findings of Clarke and Kornberg (1979), who also found the economic backgrounds of male and female party leaders to be quite similar. Moreover, this pattern is important as it suggests that rather than representing counties that are notably different or representing different political belief structures, male and female chairs appear to have quite similar political beliefs and come from quite similar counties. This similarity casts significant doubt on the assertion that it is differences in their background, rather than in their gender, that caused the response patterns observed.

The second comparison, shown in Table 4.8, reveals that women party chairs and the sample of potential women candidates have quite similar responses to the measures that were asked of both groups. In the personality trait indexes, in estimating the chances of women candidates, and in the gender of the people they would advocate as state legislative candidates, women party chairs and potential women candidates offer quite similar responses, again producing no statistically significant differences. The relevance of this comparison is that the potential women candidates represent a much larger group, encompassing a great geographic and political diversity in the four states studied. Thus, their similarity with women party chairs adds further credence to the claim that it is not the counties women party chairs represent or the political backgrounds they offer; it is their gender that produces their distinctive response pattern (in comparison with male party chairs) and ultimately produces support for the outgroup effect.

An alternate interpretation of the data, however, also deserves some attention. The variation between male and female party chair responses has been utilized as evidence of the importance of the outgroup effect in party chair perceptions. Perhaps, instead of providing strong evidence for a widespread outgroup effect, the differences shown between male and female party chairs reflect only the bias of women to prefer women candidates and unbiased male party chairs. In other words, many of the results illustrated a difference between male and female party chairs, but is to be different from female party chairs inherent evidence of bias? If male party chairs offered unbiased assessments while women party chairs offered estimates that were biased against men, it would likely produce the same patterns reported here.

Further examination of the evidence does not support this counter-explanation. In isolation from comparison with women, male party chairs show a consistent

Table 4.7
Background by Gender of Party Chair

	Male	Female
Chairs' Political Setting		
Party of Chair (% Republican)	51	49
Percentage Women State Legislators	14	14
Ideology of Chair	5.0	4.9[a]
Ideology of Electorate	4.8	4.7[a]
Party Strength in Electorate	4.5	4.4[a]
Party Organization Strength	2.6	2.6[b]
Chairs' Personal Demographics		
Age of Chair	54	55
Race of Chair (% white)	96	100
Demographics of Chairs' Districts		
Income (mean income in 1,000s)	39	36
Education (% college degree)	24	22
Age (% over 55)	21	25
Race (% white)	78	77

N = 280.

[a]Seven-point scales Ideology: (1 = Very Liberal, 7 = Very Conservative); Party Strength: (1 = Strong Democratic, 7 = Strong Republican).
[b]Five-point scale (1 = Very Strong, 5 = Not Strong).
Note: None of the relationships reach statistical significance at (p < .10).

preference for male candidates, suggesting it is not merely a function of being compared with women party chairs that makes male party chairs look like they prefer ingroup over outgroup candidates.

If the findings are simply a function of an outgroup effect in women's behavior and not men's, women's responses should reveal evidence of outgroup bias while men's would not. For example, the occupation evaluation should show women favoring their own occupational group, while unbiased men should display no particular preference for candidates most similar to themselves. Instead, when the responses to the occupation evaluation are broken down by gender, both men and women appear quite partial to their own occupations (mean rating: male chairs = 5.6/female chairs = 5.4; percent rating their occupation in the top half: male chairs = 85%/female chairs = 85%, differences statistically insignificant). The great similarity shown indicates both men and women have a predilection for same occupation candidates, suggesting both men and women prefer ingroup over outgroup candidates.

Table 4.8
Comparison of Women Chair Responses with Potential Women Candidates

Personality Trait Index
Female Trait Index[a]
Female Chairs	3.4
Candidates	3.5

Male Trait Index
Female Chairs	1.7
Candidates	1.6

N = 310.

Estimated Electoral Chance of Women Candidates
	Chance of Success[b]
Party Chairs	57
Candidates	59

N = 322.

Women Legislative Candidate Chances Over Time
Gender of Chair	% Reporting Little Change
Chairs	75
Candidates	73

N = 322.

Gender of Future State Legislative Recruits
	# of Women in Top Five	% Female Top Choice
Party Chairs	2.2	47
Candidates	2.3	51

N = 321.

[a]Scores represent the cumulative average response to five personality traits. The most favorable score possible was 7, the least favorable score -7.
[b]on a scale from 0 to 100 (0 = no chance, 100 = certain victory)
Note: None of the relationships reach statistical significance at p < .10.

Does the finding that women party chairs seem to be affected by the outgroup effect change or affect the results presented to this point? Does the apparent lack of a neutral benchmark for comparison negate these conclusions? It does not because the intent of this chapter is not to conclusively demonstrate the amount and ramifications of bias, but rather to attempt to distinguish between two possible perceptual effects. The evidence consistently supports the conclusion that party chairs exhibit an outgroup perceptual effect, in that they are drawn to candidates more like themselves. This chapter represents a first step, indicating the apparent pervasiveness of the outgroup effect examined in the aggregate.

One further retort to this conclusion would be to question the significance of this finding given the existing evidence in support of the outgroup effect (Jones, Wood, and Quattrone 1981; Judd and Park 1988; Mackie and Worth 1989; Carpenter 1993). However, the evidence presented here cannot be dismissed as merely repackaging the conventional wisdom, for two reasons. First, there is little consistency, much less consensus, on the types of bias or even whether women face bias when they pursue leadership positions (Eagly, Makhijani, and Klonsky 1992). Second, while studies of outgroup effects have been typically performed in a variety of laboratory or unnatural settings (see Funder 1987), this research involves the attitudes and behaviors of significant political actors in the real world. Party chair decisions, and their influence on potential women candidates, are factors shaping the government. To argue that they are affected by the outgroup effect is, then, neither redundant nor insignificant.

SUMMARY AND CONCLUSIONS

The value of studying gender bias among party chairs could be challenged by previous work which suggests that party leaders are not biased against women. The results of the survey of potential women state legislative candidates indicates something quite different. Not only did a majority respond that discrimination exists in the recruitment process, a significant number provided personal illustrations of the bias they had experienced.

If bias exists, what motivates such bias? Numerous evaluations were utilized to shed light on whether the distribution effect or the outgroup effect influenced party chair behavior. In the occupation ranking, the personality trait scale, women's electoral chances in different situations, women's chances over time, and in the gender of future candidates, party chairs did not strongly respond to the distribution of the person's traits in politics. However, party chairs displayed a consistent and significant preference for ingroup members over outgroup members.

The comparative support for female candidates and traits from male party chairs and female party chairs, the weak correlation between distribution and evaluation, and the consistent support for one's ingroup over one's outgroup all fail to provide support for the distribution effect, and all are consistent with the outgroup effect. In other words, all tests are consistent with the notion that party chairs make assumptions of positive similarity with ingroup members and not with the outgroup, exaggerate traits of the outgroup, and fail to individuate (or homogenize) the outgroup, potentially to the great detriment of women.

NOTES

1. California Republican.

2. New Jersey Democrat.

3. New Jersey Republican.

4. California Democrat.

5. Ohio Democrat.

6. Tennessee Republican.

7. New Jersey Republican.

8. Statistical significance in this and the following comparisons refers to 2-tailed t-tests.

9. Sniderman et al. (1991) find that describing an African American as a dependable worker tends to reduce or eliminate prejudiced reactions to that individual because the description violates the stereotypes of many respondents. In this situation, identifying the woman candidate as an incumbent or as emphasizing "mainstream issues" may violate the stereotype party leaders have of women candidates; thus it is necessary to provide the challenger and "women's issues" categories to prevent the description from artificially lowering displayed bias against women.

10. On the tendency to associate women candidates with certain issues, see Huddy and Terkildsen (1993a), Alexander and Andersen (1993), and Kahn and Goldenberg (1991).

11. The variance of the 12 estimates from each individual was first calculated, then the average variance for party chairs was calculated by determining the average of those scores. This method was chosen, instead of simply using the traditional aggregate variance, because the purpose was to try to isolate whether individuals recognized differences in the scenarios presented them. For example, if one party chairs gave an estimate of 10% for each situation, and another gave an estimate of 60% for each situation, these figures would produce variance as it is traditionally calculated. By individually calculating variance, and then averaging the scores, this situation would produce no variance, which accurately reflects the estimates given.

12. Although it is hypothesized that party leader attitudes influence the number of women elected in their district, the idea of the distribution effect is that the number of women elected influences party leaders' attitudes, an apparent tautology. This can be resolved by making a distinction between personal experience with women candidates and overall observation of women candidacies. Party leaders would be expected to observe their state's overall record

of electing women, yet they could have no influence outside their own county. One would expect the number of women elected overall to influence distribution-based attitudes. Those attitudes would then be expected to influence the number of women sought to run for winnable seats in the party leader's district. This conception of the process would ideally be tested by time-series data, but in a one-time survey one is forced to rely on a recall question. However, the reliance on recall does not prevent this question from being informative. If party leaders cannot exactly recall their opinions of women candidates 10 years ago, they can probably assess the relative direction of their feelings on the election of women over the course of recent time.

5

The Determinants of Bias

The legislature in Sacramento is filled with carpet bagger puppet boys . . . instead of qualified women. Why? We have a serious problem, and the party people are guilty.

In rather colorful verbiage, one California Republican woman candidate, with this comment in her survey, suggests the central question in the study of bias in recruitment. Why? Why would party leaders seek to avoid female legislative candidacies? Why would party leaders even consider less capable candidates if they had access to others? The results presented in Chapter 4 offer rather strong evidence that the perceptions of the party chairs appear to be colored by factors outside of objectivity. Specifically, their pattern of reactions to potential candidate traits appears quite consistent with the outgroup effect.

Fully considered, however, the "why" question is obviously not completely addressed by identifying the malady, as the question merely shifts to become "why do party chairs display this form of perceptual bias?" If the outgroup effect is influencing male party chairs to favor men, where and why do these biases occur? This chapter will endeavor to examine the correlates and determinants of the outgroup and distribution effects in an effort to better understand the where and why of their existence. Toward that end, this chapter first offers an individual-level measure of the outgroup and distribution effects. Then, a review of psychological findings pertaining to the correlates of bias is presented. The third, and largest, component of the chapter is the presentation of the data pertaining to the determinants of the outgroup and distribution effects.

INDIVIDUAL-LEVEL MEASURES

The conclusions in Chapter 4 regarding the prevalence of the outgroup and distribution effects were based on aggregate patterns. Comparisons were made on key dimensions, such as between male and female party chairs, and between those from areas with larger and smaller distributions of women officeholders.

Extending these results, by evaluating county party chair perceptions on the individual level, serves two key purposes. First, replicating this process on the individual level will solidify confidence in the earlier conclusions. If the aggregate conclusions are sound, they should be equally apparent when the data are analyzed on the individual level. Second, individual-level assessments of bias provide the necessary cases and variance to facilitate an examination of the correlates or determinants of bias.

The first step in such a process is to create a score for each individual respondent reflecting their tendency to make evaluations consistent with the outgroup effect and a score representing their tendency to make evaluations consistent with the distribution effect. The measures that provided the foundation for the aggregate assessment of perceptions can also be adapted to use in creating an individual-level score. There were five major tests discussed in Chapter 4, involving occupation, personality traits, women candidates' chances over time, women candidates' chances in different situations, and the gender of future candidates. Basing the bias scores just on the occupation and trait tests offers two relevant advantages. First, these scores are the least susceptible of the five tests to desirability effects, since gender is not explicitly part of the question (see Jackman and Muha 1984). Second, the validity of the outgroup and distribution scores can then be assessed by comparing the scores to responses for the three remaining measures. Given that the theory underlying this study is that broad perceptual biases exist that happen to have specific ramifications for potential women candidates, utilizing more broad, non-explicitly gender-based measures should predict reactions to women candidates in specific situations.

Utilizing the occupation and traits tests, the outgroup score is therefore based on the respondents' tendency to positively evaluate occupations and traits associated with themselves. A three-point scale was created; respondents who rated candidates with their occupation as being the most desirable of the seven occupations listed, and who rated candidates with traits associated with their gender as being more desirable than traits associated with the other gender, receive a score of 2. Respondents whose responses fit one, but not both, of these categories receive a score of 1. Respondents who did not rate candidates from their occupation as most desirable, and who did not rate candidate traits associated with their gender as being more desirable, receive a score of 0.

The distribution score is based on the tendency to positively evaluate occupations and traits that are prevalent in politics. Respondents who rated candidates who were lawyers as the most desirable of the seven occupations listed,[1] and who rated traits more widely associated with politicians as being more desirable than traits thought more rarely held among politicians, receive a score of 2. Respondents whose responses fit one, but not both, of these categories receive a score of 1. Respondents who did not rate candidates from the legal profession as

Table 5.1
Frequencies of Perceptual Bias Scores

Outgroup

Score	n	%
0 (no bias)	38	14
1	92	33
2 (high bias)	150	53

N = 280.

Distribution

Score	n	%
0 (no bias)	178	64
1	93	33
2 (high bias)	9	3

N = 280.

most desirable, and who did not rate candidate traits more widely associated with politicians as being more desirable, receive a score of 0.

The scores produced by this operationalization of the outgroup and distribution effects offer a picture of perceptions that is quite consistent with the one drawn in the previous chapter. As Table 5.1 illustrates, the majority of respondents are classified as being affected by the outgroup effect. Specifically, only 14% receive a 0 score (indicating the absence of the outgroup effect), while a stunning 53% receive a 2. Conversely, only 36% show signs of the distribution effect, with a paltry 3% receiving the more pronounced score of 2.

While this consistency with previous conclusions is relevant, a far more significant question remains concerning whether these scores actually indicate what they are intended to measure. If these scores are valid, then, as the outgroup score rises, the county party chairs should show a greater tendency to support candidates from their own gender. The distribution score should indicate whether there is a relationship between the prevalence of women and the evaluation of women with those who receive higher scores demonstrating a stronger relationship.

On a number of key measures tested, the outgroup score does predict the reaction to female candidates. For male party chairs, higher outgroup scores are indicative of a significantly lower assessment of the likelihood of a woman winning elective office, significantly less variance in the estimates for women in different scenarios (indicating inattention to individuating information), and having significantly fewer women in mind for future candidacies (Table 5.2). For female party chairs, higher outgroup scores are indicative of a significantly higher assessment of the likelihood of a woman winning elective office, significantly more variance in the estimates for women in different scenarios (indicating greater attention to individuating information), and having significantly more women in mind for future candidacies. In sum, higher outgroup scores appear to be quite valid indicators of one's propensity to favor ingroup candidates over outgroup candidates.

Testing the validity of the distribution score hinges not on the gender of the respondent, but on the distribution of women in politics that the respondent observes. As Table 5.3 indicates, respondents with a higher distribution score display a greater connection between the distribution of women in office and their evaluations of women as candidates. Conversely, those with a 0 distribution score reveal little connection between the number of women legislators in their state and their assessments of women's chances, the variance in those assessments, or the number of women future candidates they have in mind.

Both the outgroup score and the distribution score, therefore, appear to function as adequate indicators of the respondents' susceptibility to these effects. What, then, distinguishes those with low scores from those with high scores? In other words, what are the determinants of biased perceptions?

Past research offers a voluminous, if sometimes inconsistent, array of evidence on what potential variables should be examined as correlates of perceptual bias. For organizational simplicity, the two major categories of variables that will be examined can be labeled personal and political. Personal variables center on the experiences and background of the party chair, while political variables include the professional and electoral situation in which the chair operates. Previous research is not well developed enough to provide significant foundation for distinguishing between variables that would encourage the outgroup effect from variables that would encourage the distribution effect.

Therefore, rather than separately presenting hypotheses for the outgroup and distribution effects, the discussion that follows centers on correlates of biased thinking--in other words, the correlates of thinking that might be conducive to either or both of the forms of bias studied here.

Table 5.2
Relationship between Outgroup Score and Perceptions of Women Candidates

Male Party Chairs

Outgroup Score	Likelihood of Woman Candidate Victory[a]	Variance in Women Candidate Assessment[b]	Number of Women Considered as Future Candidates[c]
0	53	469	2.1
1	50	382	1.7
2	44	333	1.1
Significance	.01	.01	.01

N = 233.

Female Party Chairs

Outgroup Score	Likelihood of Woman Candidate Victory	Variance in Women Candidate Assessment	Number of Women Considered as Future Candidates
0	47	359	1.6
1	54	465	1.9
2	59	557	2.4
Significance	.10	.10	.10

N = 44.

[a]on a scale from 0 to 100 (0 = no chance, 100 = certain victory).
[b]derived from estimate of woman candidate's chances in 12 electoral scenarios.
[c]number of women out of five top future legislative candidates.

Table 5.3
Distribution Scores and the Correlation between Prevalence of Women Candidates and Perceptions of Women Candidates

Distribution Score	Likelihood of Woman Candidate Victory	Variance in Women Candidate Assessment	Number of Women Considered as Future Candidates
0	.04	-.09	.22
1	.23	.08	.29
2	.56	.55	.76

N = 273.

Note: scores have been recoded to make the expected relationship positive for all three variables.

Political Determinants

Outcome dependency. Outcome dependency is thought to discourage perceptual bias (Erber and Fiske 1984). According to this logic, the motivation to be accurate is greater when success hinges on it. In this context, relevant indicators include whether the party chairs' state legislative districts are winnable and whether they are competitive. The closeness of the electoral race indicates the importance of the quality of the candidates. In a closely contested district, the outcome may hinge on the quality of the candidate. Meanwhile, the candidate should have less influence on the outcome in districts where there is a great imbalance of party strength. Therefore, in close or at least winnable districts, party chairs should have greater motivation to accurately assess potential candidates.

As an indicator for this and the subsequent concepts outlined, the survey of county party chairs will be utilized. With regard to outcome dependency, party chairs were asked to rate the relative strength of their party and the opposition party in their local state legislative districts.

Accountability. Accountability is also thought to encourage accuracy motivation (Tetlock 1983). Those who will or could be held responsible for their decisions should take more care in assessing the situation, or in this case, assessing candidates. For party chairs, one would imagine that those chairs who are new to their position will feel more accountable to produce results and to please their fellow party members. More veteran chairs would have a longer history on which to be judged and would therefore likely feel less accountable for each individual decision they make about a candidate. In addition to tenure as chair, effort expended on recruiting also likely relates to accountability. The more effort the party chair puts into recruiting, especially with regard to imposing his or her will over the process, the more they will be associated with the success or failure of the candidates. Thus, the accountability theory predicts that to the extent party chairs are more involved, they will display less perceptual bias.

Again turning to the survey, party chairs were asked how long they had held the office of county party chair and how much effort they personally expended in recruiting candidates for the state legislature.

Rigidity. Those who are more certain in their decisions tend to question their own thinking less and are more susceptible to believing in the infallibility of their initial conclusions (Jussim 1990). Party chairs provided assessments of how certain they were of the quality of party candidates and reported whether they took an active role in discouraging unacceptable candidates. These are both presumably good indicators of rigidity as those who indicate that they are quite expert in their assessments and those who indicate they frequently discourage unacceptable candidates seem to be expressing a certainty in their actions.

Power over outcomes. Where people have power over outcomes, they tend to display more perceptual bias (Hacker 1951). When people can enforce their decisions, they likely experience less pressure to change or to accept counter-stereotypical information. Party chairs who have more power over candidate selection thus would be able to continually utilize their preferences and face little incentive to accept candidates that do not fit their preferred image. Party chairs who have less influence over candidate selection will likely face more candidates who do not fit their ideal image. As less powerful party chairs face a diversity of candidates, they have more opportunities to update or expand their perceptions of acceptable candidates.

The condition of the party in terms of the strength of its organization and its strength in the electorate also indicates how much power the chair has. The less developed the organization and the less likely the party is to win, the less power the chair enjoys over the ultimate outcome and the less perceptual bias we would expect to see according to the theory. Party chairs provided their estimates for both indicators of party strength and commented on their role in the recruiting process.

Time. Time pressure likely increases stereotypic perceptions (Fiske and Taylor 1991, 161). People with more time to consider their evaluations are likely to have a higher motivation for accuracy, as time permits them to be more careful. Those rushed to make a decision are more likely to fall prey to initial inclinations, which are more prone to be shaped by perceptual bias. Party chairs who report that they have sufficient time to find and evaluate candidates should therefore be less likely to rely on perceptual biases and should be more capable of attending to individuating information.

Some of these concepts, such as rigidity, are presented as political determinants though they could potentially be labeled personal. Given the focus of the indicators used in this examination, however, they more accurately fit the political category.

Future efforts, focusing exclusively on exploring determinants of elite bias, might endeavor to create both political and personal indicators of such concepts.

Personal Determinants

Exposure. Among the personal factors that might be of significance in understanding the pattern of party chair perceptions are their age, family, education, occupation, and personal ideology. For lack of a generally used shorthand, these personal variables are treated as indicators of the exposure of the respondent to a diversity of people, ideas, and experiences. The expectation is that influences that tend to expose people to more, to a wider range of experiences or ideas, will decrease their likelihood of relying on perceptual biases (Bennett and Bennett 1992).

As Fiske, Kinder, and Larter describe, "People draw heavily on accumulated experience to aid their understanding. The more experience they have, the more easily and thoroughly they can assimilate new information" (1983, 382). Party chairs with more exposure to diversity--more experience with it, according to the logic of their work--would be expected to more easily process and utilize information, especially inconsistent information, about unfamiliar candidates (Fiske, Kinder, and Larter 1983; Fiske, Lau, and Smith 1990). Thus, perceptual bias would be less likely because the party chairs would attend to individuating or inconsistent information and utilize that when making an evaluation.

Party chairs can certainly be thought of as experts in recruiting and candidate evaluation. However, to be an expert in one area does not necessarily accompany great exposure, experience, or expertise in dealing with unique or unfamiliar situations, such as when the first woman candidate comes forward. Significantly, McGraw and Pinney (1990) find that domain-specific expertise does not relieve one from falling prey to selective memory effects, but that greater political sophistication does. In other words, even though party chairs have an expertise in recruiting, this trait will not prevent them from utilizing hypothesis-confirming behavior when they interact with unfamiliar potential candidates. It is only when they have a larger cadre of exposure that they would be expected to attend well to both consistent and discrepant information concerning such a candidate. Therefore, the expectation is that party chairs who have experienced more diversity will be more capable of processing information about different candidates and will be less likely to rely on perceptual bias.

Age is obviously related to the time and conditions under which one was socialized, making it an important component of exposure to ideas. Those who are older are likely to be less prepared to evaluate a diversity of candidates and more prone to biased perceptions, because their socialization and life experiences were less likely to condition them for the wide range of people who now hold positions of influence (Bennett and Bennett 1992; Thornton, Alwin, and Camburn 1983). Education is also thought to be a factor in decreasing perceptual biases as education also brings with it access to new ideas and people (Bennett and Bennett 1992; Welch and Sigelman 1982). Party chairs were asked to indicate their year of birth as well as the highest level of education they attained.

The family situation is certainly relevant as the first example most people receive of gender roles. Scholars hypothesize that those who are exposed to active or independent women at an early age will be more accepting of women's political activities later in life (Thornton, Alwin, and Camburn 1983). Toward that end, chairs were asked which members, if any, of their family were active in politics and influenced their interest in politics. For the purposes of this examination, chairs will be divided into those who reported having an influential female family member (mother, grandmother, or aunt) and those who did not.

Choice of occupation, and the resulting experiences it exposes one to, is considered to be a most significant adult socializing experience (Brooks 1995; Andersen and Cook 1985; Ferber, Huber, and Spitze 1979). Psychologists write of the concept of occupational prestige, which taps notions of exclusivity and power (Yoder 1994; Hartman et al. 1988; Palisi and Canning 1991). Such exclusivity and power indicates the degree to which a person can control their atmosphere or the degree to which they can control the types and traits of people surrounding them (Arrighi-Merz 1991; Winter, Stewart, and McClelland 1977). As such, chairs who have higher occupational prestige will be expected to have more constrained exposure and display more perceptual bias.

Personal ideology is thought to be another significant predictor of attitudes toward the role of women. Conservatives, because of their views on the proper role for women or because of their greater attachment to tradition, have been found to be less supportive of women's activity in politics (Welch and Sigelman 1982; Bennett and Bennett 1992). According to this argument, conservative party chairs should have less experience with women in non-traditional roles and be less open to change in general. In the process, conservatism should result in party chairs having less exposure to diversity and more attitudes influenced by perceptual bias.

Again, all of the personal determinants can be thought of as indicators of exposure. Those who have been exposed to more countervailing ideas should be less likely to utilize biased perceptions because they are more capable of dealing with inconsistent information (Fiske, Kinder, and Larter 1983; McGraw and Pinney 1990). Thus, exposure should make party chairs more capable of evaluating a person instead of relying on their evaluation of a category or group the person resembles.

OUTGROUP SCORES

Bivariate Relationships

As an initial test, the bivariate relationships between the outgroup scores and the predictors outlined in this chapter will be examined. For ease of presentation, and given that the expectations have been established, the statistical significance of all bivariate relationships will be measured with a 1-tailed t-test. The overall

Table 5.4
Hypothesized Predictors of Perceptual Bias

Category	Indicators	Operationalization and Predicted Effect on Bias
Outcome Dependency	winnable race	likely to contend (dichotomous 0 = no, 1 = yes)(-)
	competitiveness of district	competitiveness on three-point scale (1 = low)(-)
Accountability	time as chair	first year as chair(-)
	recruiting effort	effort on three-point scale (1 = low) (-)
Rigidity	time as chair	first year as chair (-)
	confidence in candidate assessments	confidence on three-point scale (1 = low)(+)
	likelihood of discouraging candidates (unqualified)	discourage unqualified candidates (dichotomous 0 = no, 1 = yes)(+)
	likelihood of discouraging candidates (poor profile)	discourage poor profile (dichotomous 0 = no, 1 = yes)(+)
Power	recruiting power	decision power (dichotomous 0 = no, 1 = yes)(+)
	strength of party organization	strength on five-point scale (1 = lowest) (+)
	strength of party in electorate	expect to win (dichotomous 0 = no, 1=yes)(+)
Time	Time to evaluate potential recruits	time (dichotomous 0 = no, 1 = yes)(-)
Exposure	age	year of birth (-)
	family	politically influence women family member (dichotomous 0 = no, 1 = yes)(-)
	education	highest level completed (1 = HS, 2 = College, 3 = Advance Degree)(-)
	occupation	occupational prestige on five-point scale (1 = lowest) (+)
	ideology	seven-point scale (1 = liberal) (+)

mean outgroup score is 1.4, therefore any measure with a score below 1.4 is associated with a decrease in outgroup scores, and any measure above 1.4 is associated with an increase. Table 5.4 summarizes the indicators that will be used and the expected relationships.

Table 5.5
Outcome Dependency Effect on Outgroup Score

Competitiveness of District	Outgroup Score	n
LOW	1.5	63
MEDIUM	1.3	60
HIGH	1.1**	152

Winnable Race	Outgroup Score	n
NO	1.5	56
YES	1.4	224

**difference significant at p < .01

Political Variables

To assess the effects of outcome dependency, two related indicators are utilized. The first is a three-point competitiveness scale in which party chairs rated the electoral competitiveness of their county's state legislative districts. The second measure is a simple dichotomous variable separating cases where the chair reported his or her party had little or no chance of winning in their districts from parties where the chair thought they would or might win. The distinction between these two measures is that the competitiveness variable taps uncertainty without regard to which party is advantaged, while the second measure will more directly examine the effect of being incapable of winning.

According to the outcome dependency logic, both the competitiveness and the chance of winning measures should show a relationship where greater competition leads to less bias. In other words, where the districts are more competitive or where the party chairs think there is some chance of victory, lower outgroup scores should emerge.

As revealed in Table 5.5, the competitiveness measure has a rather clear and statistically significant relationship ($p < .01$) with the outgroup score. Those in the most competitive districts have the lowest outgroup score, while those in the least competitive districts have the highest outgroup score. The second measure, regarding whether the party could win, showed that being an electoral longshot was associated with a slightly higher outgroup score. Together, these two findings suggest that outcome dependency or electoral uncertainty does reduce outgroup perceptions, and that the key distinction is not whether the party is quite likely to win or to lose, but rather whether the party's fate is certain or uncertain.

Table 5.6
Accountability Effect on Outgroup Score

	Outgroup	
First Year as Chair	Score	n
1958-1980	1.5	46
1981-1987	1.4	57
1988-1991	1.3	70
1992-1993	1.3	51
1994-	1.2*	52
	Outgroup	
Recruiting Effort	Score	n
LOW	1.5	138
MEDIUM	1.2	53
HIGH	1.1*	89

*difference significant at p < .05

Accountability was measured with two simple questions concerning the party chair: how long have they held the chair's position? and how much effort do they personally put into recruiting? Effort was assessed by asking the chair to rate their activity in recruiting on a three-point scale. It is expected that newer chairs and those who invest more personally into recruiting will feel more accountable and thus will display less outgroup bias.

Both effort and length of tenure display clear, statistically significant relationships (p < .05) with the outgroup score in the expected direction (Table 5.6). The most accountable, the highest effort and shortest tenure categories, produce mean outgroups scores of 1.1 and 1.2 respectively. Meanwhile, the least accountable, lowest effort and longest tenure, produce mean outgroup scores of 1.5. The relationships between outgroup scores and these accountability measures lend strong support to the position that added accountability reduces perceptual bias.

Three political measures were used as indicators of cognitive rigidity. In addition to the chairs' confidence in her or his assessments, two variables concerning the likelihood of discouraging candidates were incorporated. Confidence was measured with a three-point scale asking the chair how much confidence the chair had in his or her assessment of potential candidates for office. Chairs were also asked yes or no questions on whether they engage in discouraging candidates they consider to be unqualified and whether they have discouraged candidates because the candidate did not fit the desired profile. Discouraging candidates and expressing a lot of confidence in one's assessments of candidates are intuitively appealing measures of the rigidity with which chairs approach their jobs.

Table 5.7
Cognitive Rigidity Effect on Outgroup Score

Confidence in Candidate Assessments	Outgroup Score	n
LOW	1.1	69
MEDIUM	1.3	85
HIGH	1.5*	118

Discourage Unqualified Candidates	Outgroup Score	n
NO	1.4	104
YES	1.5	171

Discourage Poor Profile Candidates	Outgroup Score	n
NO	1.4	233
YES	1.6*	42

*difference significant at $p < .05$

The results, presented in Table 5.7, are largely consistent with expectations. Greater confidence in assessments and discouraging candidates that do not fit the ideal profile both result in higher outgroup bias scores. Discouraging unqualified candidates also is associated with an increased outgroup score; however, it is not a statistically significant relationship. In sum, all three indicators of rigidity are in the expected direction, with two of the three statistically significant, thus offering support to the position that greater rigidity is associated with more outgroup bias.

Three measures related to power over outcomes are used. The first is a measure of the party chair's power over the recruiting process. Party chairs were asked an open-ended question concerning their role in the recruitment process. The responses have been coded to create a simple dichotomous distinction between chairs who indicated they had a dominant role in the recruitment process from those who indicated they played a more secondary role. The other two measures are indicative of the strength of the party. First, a five-point scale of party organizational strength, and second, a dichotomous measure concerning whether the party chair expects his or her party to win the next state legislative race in their county, are utilized. All three measures are strongly related to power over outcomes as they indicate how much control the party chair has, first, over the

Table 5.8
Power over Outcome Effect on Outgroup Score

Recruiting Power	Outgroup Score	n
NO	1.5	113
YES	1.2**	167

Strength of _Party Organization_	Outgroup Score	n
NOT STRONG	1.2	15
2	1.2	43
3	1.2	81
4	1.4	84
VERY STRONG	1.5	51

Expect to Win Next _Legislative Election_	Outgroup Score	n
NO	1.3	130
YES	1.4	146

**difference significant at $p < .01$

selection of the candidate, and then over the fate of the candidate. Obviously, the weaker the party or the expectation of losing indicates a lack of power over the ultimate outcome. Given the power over outcomes theory posits more power should lead to more perceptual bias; stronger parties, a higher likelihood of winning, and more power in the recruiting process should therefore be associated with higher outgroup bias scores.

The results, presented in Table 5.8, do not support the power over outcomes theory. Strength of party and expectation of winning are not significantly related to outgroup bias scores. More startlingly, power in recruiting is significantly related to outgroup scores, but in the opposite of the expected direction. Those with more recruiting power, according to the data, have lower outgroup scores. Obviously, the three relationships offer no support for the position that power over outcomes increases outgroup bias.

Table 5.9
Time Pressure Effect on Outgroup Score

Time to Evaluate Recruits	Outgroup Score	n
NO	1.6	96
YES	1.3*	176

*difference significant at p < .05

Time pressure is measured simply with a dichotomous variable developed from open-ended responses to the recruiting process question. The variable was created by distinguishing those who indicated that they and their party had sufficient time to find new candidates from those who indicated in any way that the recruitment process was rushed. According to the theory, greater time pressure should encourage the use of biased perceptions, while having adequate time should encourage the use of individuating information.

The relationship between time pressure and outgroup scores is provided in Table 5.9. The relationship is in the expected direction and is statistically significant (p < .05). Party chairs who have more time to deal with potential recruits have an average score of 1.3, while those who have less time have an average score of 1.6, offering support to the time hypothesis.

Personal Variables

The personal background variables all have some relationship to exposure. Variables examined here include year of birth, education, occupation, family (female family member political activity), and ideology. Again, the expectation is that influences that tend to widen party chairs' range of experiences or ideas will decrease their likelihood of relying on perceptual biases. Thus, those who are younger, more educated, have occupations with lower prestige, have politically influential female relatives, and are more liberal should display lower outgroup scores.

These expectations meet with mixed success (Table 5.10). Year of birth quite clearly displays the expected relationship. Those who were born after 1955 have an average outgroup score of 1, while those born before 1926 have an average score of 1.6, with the relationship significant at p < .05. The occupational prestige categories, based on the typology in Arrighi-Merz (1991), also lend support to the exposure hypothesis. Those with the highest prestige find themselves above the mean in outgroup scores, while those with the lowest prestige, and theoretically the highest exposure, have a quite dramatically lower outgroup score than the other categories.

Table 5.10
Exposure/Personal Background Effect on Outgroup Score

	Outgroup	
Year of Birth	Score	n
1912-1926	1.6	45
1927-1945	1.4	57
1946-1954	1.3	147
1955-1972	1.0*	27

Politically Influential	Outgroup	
Female Family Member	Score	n
NO	1.4	224
YES	1.3	56

	Outgroup	
Education	Score	n
HIGH SCHOOL	1.2	101
COLLEGE	1.4	73
ADVANCED/PROFESSIONAL		
DEGREE	1.5*	103

	Outgroup	
Occupational Prestige	Score	n
LOWEST	0.7	29
2	1.1	14
3	1.4	93
4	1.4	49
HIGHEST	1.5**	87

	Outgroup	
Ideology	Score	n
VERY LIBERAL	1.1	14
2	1.5	23
3	1.4	30
MODERATE	1.5	67
5	1.3	52
6	1.4	59
VERY CONSERVATIVE	1.4	32

**difference significant at $p < .01$
*difference significant at $p < .05$

Family and ideology did not provide as clear results. Having a politically influential female family member was associated with a decrease in outgroup scores, but the difference was very slight. Ideology, on the other hand, produced almost no discernable pattern.

Perhaps most interestingly, the relationship between outgroup score and education is significant and in the unexpected direction. Instead of higher education making party chairs less prone to perceptual bias, the results here show that party chairs with an advanced degree had an average outgroup score of 1.5, while those with a bachelor's degree averaged 1.4, and those whose highest level of education was a high school degree had an average outgroup score of 1.2.

How can education, widely thought of as an experience capable of reducing bias, appear to be not only unhelpful but hurtful? Jackman and Muha (1984) would argue that the expectation and findings in support of the connection between education and non-biased behavior are largely artifacts derived from the educated person's advantage in the survey setting. Jackman and Muha argue that educated people can better spot questions that may reflect poorly on themselves and can modify their responses to fit the socially desirable position. In this survey, specifically in the items that went into creating the outgroup score, the purpose and implications of the questions were hidden from the respondents. In the process, educated respondents could not modify their responses to fit social desirability since it would not have been clear to them that they needed to do that nor how they could do that. These results, then, are quite consistent with Jackman and Muha's finding that the educated may be more rigid and more likely to exclude others.

Nonetheless, the political variables offer support to four theories: outcome dependency, accountability, rigidity, and time pressure as influences on outgroup bias. Personal variables, such as year of birth and occupation, offered some support, but other variables were inconsistent with the exposure theory.

Multivariate Analysis

Ultimately, a more rigorous test of these hypotheses is available by regressing the outgroup score on the various determinants discussed. The regression results are of particular interest in assessing the determinants of the outgroup effect since most psychological studies of bias focus on a single factor and do not have the capability of testing the veracity of competing theories (but see Agnew et al. 1993).

In addition to the previously discussed variables, further controls of interest have been added including the gender of the party chair, the party of the chair, the ideology of the district, and three dummy variables meant to capture differences in the states under study. Party, ideology, and the state dummy variables allow for factors larger than the chairs' immediate situations to be included. If party chairs are responding not because of their ideas, but because of the larger political factors that they feel they must conform to, then these variables should be important determinants of outgroup scores. Party chair gender is added out of obvious curiosity, although there is reason to suspect it will not provide theoretically interesting results (Bennett 1986; Gurin 1985; Simon and Landis 1989). The regression model is presented in Table 5.11.

The outgroup score regression model offers further support for the importance of outcome dependency and rigidity. The two outcome dependency measures, competitiveness of district and being an electoral longshot, both emerge as important variables. According to the regression model, a change to longshot status or from the most competitive to the least competitive district adds approximately .9 to the outgroup score. Support for the rigidity theory exists in the performance of the confidence in candidate assessments indicator, which, according to the model, can add .24 to the outgroup score when changed from low to high.

Accountability and time pressure, which appeared to be relevant concerns in the bivariate analysis, both fail to make a significant impact in the regression model.

Perhaps the most interesting difference between the bivariate and multivariate results occurs for power over outcomes. Here, unlike in the bivariate analysis, support emerges for the original hypothesis that added power would be associated with more perceptual bias. Of the three indicators, expecting to win has the largest effect. The difference between being unsure about the electoral outcome and expecting to win accompanies an almost .7 increase in the outgroup score. Party strength, although significant only at $p < .07$, also contributes moderately, such that reduced strength reduces the outgroup score.

Why would power over outcomes be significant and in the expected direction here, but not in the bivariate analysis? Examination of the correlations between the independent variables suggests the reason might be the relationship between power over outcomes and time pressure (correlations are provided in Appendix C). Less recruiting power is associated with more time pressure ($r = .46$), and as the regression results indicate, these two features have opposite effects, with less power reducing bias and time pressure increasing it.[2] In the bivariate results, the influence of power over outcomes is clouded by its relationship with time pressure. Controlling for time pressure removes this complication and produces the hypothesized relationship: more power is accompanied by more outgroup bias.

With regard to personal background, two variables emerge significant: year of birth and occupational prestige. Moving from the oldest to the youngest reduces the outgroup score by .45, while moving from the most to the least occupational prestige reduces the outgroup score by about .7. Interestingly, education fails to contribute significantly to the equation. This suggests that the relationship between education and outgroup scores observed in the bivariate analysis (Table 5.10) may have been a product of the occupational prestige associated with each level of education (occupational prestige and education are correlated at $r = .43$). Thus, it was not that education made party chairs more prone to bias, but that increased education also increased their occupational prestige, which in turn limited their exposure and resulted in increased outgroup scores.

Finally, the added controls for party chair gender,[3] district ideology, and dummy variables representing California, New Jersey, and Ohio were not significant. This signifies that outgroup bias can be found in relatively equal proportions among men

Table 5.11
Multivariate Regression: Determinants of Outgroup Score

	B	S.E
Outcome Dependency		
Competitiveness of District(-)	-.30**	.11
Winnable Race(-)	-.85**	.001
Accountability		
Tenure as Chair(-)	.02	.04
Recruiting Effort(-)	-.12	.09
Cognitive Rigidity		
Confidence in Candidate Assessments(+)	.12*	.06
Discourage Unqualified Candidates(+)	.01	.05
Discourage Poor-Profile Candidates(+)	.11+	.08
Power over Outcome		
Recruiting Power(+)	.004	.25
Strength of Party Organization(+)	.07+	.04
Expect to Win Next Legislative Election(+)	.67**	.28
Time Pressure		
Time to Evaluate Recruits(-)	-.02	.23
Exposure/Personal Background		
Age(-)	-.15**	.06
Family(-)	-.01	.15
Education(-)	-.02	.05
Occupation(+)	.18**	.05
Ideology(+)	.04	.03
Controls		
District Ideology(+)	-.003	.046
Party(?)	.07	.15
California(?)	.03	.14
New Jersey(?)	-.24	.21
Ohio(?)	-.03	.19
Party Chair Gender(?)	.26	.20
Constant	1.17+	.60

$R^2 = .30$
N = 255.

** $p < .01$
*$p < .05$
+$p < .07$

Note: The variables are coded as they were in the bivariate analysis, with the addition of gender (1 = male, 2 = female), party (1 = Republican, 2 = Democrat), and the dummy variables for the three states (with Tennessee being used as the default). Expected direction of relationship provided next to variable name.

and women chairs, among liberal and conservative chairs, and among chairs in the four states under study.

The outgroup score regression model then offers support for the role of outcome dependency, rigidity, power over outcomes, and exposure in a model explaining 30% of the variance. The results indicate, in plain terms, that having an uncertain outcome, being less certain about one's assessments, not having power to enforce all of one's decisions, and being exposed to a greater diversity of people and ideas all decreased the propensity to utilize outgroup thinking in making assessments of potential candidates.

Given the overlap, conceptually, if not mathematically, between some of the indicators, there is obviously room for improvement in future studies that might concentrate solely on the question of the determinants of perceptual bias. In an effort to identify the forms, effects, and determinants of bias, less survey space was available here to dedicate to developing distinct indicators for every concept. Nevertheless, the results suggest the importance of outcome dependency, rigidity, power over outcomes, and exposure. Perhaps even more robust are the two main patterns that led to these conclusions. First, three of the six statistically significant variables (at p < .05) are closely related to electoral competition. We see that being electorally out of it increases outgroup scores, knowing your party is going to win increases outgroup scores, and greater competition decreases outgroup scores. In short, believing the outcome is predetermined apparently creates an atmosphere conducive to bias regardless of whether victory or defeat is imminent. Close competition, on the other hand, which fosters great uncertainty about the impending outcome, represents a significant mitigating force, reducing outgroup scores.

The second interesting pattern is that the other significant variables concern the related concepts of rigidity and exposure. Quite simply, the more certain politically and the less contrariant examples one has experienced personally, the more a party chair is susceptible to utilizing outgroup bias.

DISTRIBUTION SCORES

Bivariate Relationships

This section presents the bivariate relationships for distribution scores, created with the same logic and operationalization used to study outgroup scores. It should be noted that because there is less variance in the distribution scores (that is, fewer chairs displayed distribution bias), it will be somewhat more difficult to account for its determinants. The statistical significance of all bivariate relationships will again be measured with a 1-tailed t-test. The overall mean distribution score is .49, therefore any measure with a score below .49 is associated with a decrease in distribution scores, and any measure above .49 is associated with an increase.

Political Variables

As revealed in Table 5.12, both measures of outcome dependency,

Table 5.12
Outcome Dependency Effect on Distribution Score

Competitiveness of District	Distribution Score	n
LOW	0.60	63
MEDIUM	0.36	60
HIGH	0.44+	152

Winnable Race	Distribution Score	n
NO	0.51	56
YES	0.40+	224

+ difference significant at p < .10

Table 5.13
Accountability Effect on Distribution Score

First Year as Chair	Distribution Score	n
1958-1980	0.60	46
1981-1987	0.45	57
1988-1991	0.48	70
1992-1993	0.43	51
1994-	0.43	52

Recruiting Effort	Distribution Score	n
LOW	0.43	138
MEDIUM	0.55	53
HIGH	0.54	89

competitiveness and believing the race to be winnable, have the predicted effect. That is, being competitive and thinking a race is winnable lower distribution scores. Each measure is statistically significant at the p < .10 level. Again, as was the case with the outgroup effect, those for whom something is on the line, who are outcome dependent, display less bias.

Accountability, measured with effort and length of tenure as chair, does not account well for the distribution effect (Table 5.13). While tenure as chair shows a relationship that is generally in the expected direction, the relationship is not significant. The recruiting effort relationship, on the other hand, is neither in the expected direction nor very clear, as low effort has the lowest score and medium

Table 5.14
Cognitive Rigidity Effect on Distribution Score

Confidence in _Candidate Assessments_	Distribution Score	n̲
LOW	0.38	69
MEDIUM	0.51	85
HIGH	0.69**	118

Discourage _Unqualified Candidates_	Distribution Score	n̲
NO	0.48	104
YES	0.52	171

Discourage _Poor-Profile Candidates_	Distribution Score	n̲
NO	0.43	233
YES	0.61*	42

**difference significant at $p < .01$
*difference significant at $p < .05$

effort the highest score. Accountability to one's party peers, then, does not appear to be a significant influence on distribution bias.

Cognitive rigidity, as depicted in Table 5.14, has one indicator in weak agreement with the hypothesis and two indicators that offer more strong support. Confidence in candidate assessments and discouraging poor profile candidates reveal the expected relationship, with both measures reaching statistical significance. While discouraging unqualified candidates offers more qualified support, all three measures are consistent with the idea that more certainty and rigidity are associated with distribution bias.

The three measures related to power over outcomes produce inconsistent results (Table 5.15). Unlike the bivariate effect of recruiting power on outgroup scores, here recruiting power operates in the hypothesized direction. Those with power over recruiting have a higher distribution score (statistically significant at p. < .01). These party chairs can be resistant to change because they can apply their standards, here based on the distribution of women, to recruitment decisions

Table 5.15
Power over Outcome Effect on Distribution Score

	Distribution	
Recruiting Power	Score	n
NO	0.31	113
YES	0.52**	167

Strength of	Distribution	
Party Organization	Score	n
NOT STRONG	0.28	15
2	0.57	43
3	0.41	81
4	0.49	84
VERY STRONG	0.56	51

Expect to Win Next	Distribution	
Legislative Election	Score	n
NO	0.43	130
YES	0.53	146

**difference significant at p < .01

Table 5.16
Time Pressure Effect on Distribution Score

Time to	Distribution	
Evaluate Recruits	Score	n
NO	0.54	96
YES	0.46	176

without challenge. The other two indicators do not provide support, however, to the power over outcomes hypothesis. Strength of party organization reveals a rather incoherent pattern, while the expectation of winning does not strongly affect distribution scores.

Time pressure, distinguishing those chairs who had sufficient time to find new candidates from those who indicated in any way that the recruitment process was rushed, has little effect on distribution scores (Table 5.16).

Personal Variables

The personal background variables utilized include year of birth, education, occupation, family (female family member political activity), and ideology. To restate, the expectation is that influences that tend to widen party chairs' range of experiences or ideas will decrease their likelihood of relying on perceptual biases. Those who are younger, more educated, have occupations with lower prestige, have politically influential female relatives, and are more liberal should display lower distribution scores.

As was the case for the outgroup effect, these expectations meet with mixed success in explaining the relationship with distribution scores (Table 5.17). Year of birth, female family activity, and occupational prestige quite clearly display the expected relationships. Those who were born after 1955 have an average distribution score of .36, while those born before 1926 have an average score of .65, with the relationship significant at p < .05. Similarly, those in the highest occupational prestige category have a mean score of .68, while those with the lowest prestige, and presumably the highest exposure, have a quite dramatically lower distribution score than the any other category at .18. Having a politically influential female family member also produced a decrease in distribution scores.

The effect of education was in the expected direction but not significant, while the effect of ideology was inconsistent. In total, none of the personal variables are in conflict with the hypothesis that exposure produces less bias, and three of the five variables offer significant support to the premise that exposure to diversity produces less distribution based bias.

In sum, the political variables offered support to two theories: outcome dependency reduced distribution scores and rigidity was associated with higher distribution scores. Personal variables, meanwhile, offered support to the hypothesis that greater exposure reduces distribution scores.

Multivariate Relationships

As was done for the outgroup effect, a regression model testing the comparative strength of these determinants is presented in Table 5.18.

Given the greater variance in outgroup scores, the distribution score model is not surprisingly less successful than was the outgroup model in accounting for determinants of these effects (R^2 = .20 distribution score, R^2 = .30 outgroup score). Perhaps what is first notable in the distribution model is the failure of most hypotheses to contribute to our understanding of the distribution effect. Consistent and statistically significant results do emerge, however, for rigidity and exposure. Both rigidity and exposure play an important role in determining one's proclivity to be swayed by the distribution of traits. Of the exposure measures, the distance between the youngest party chairs and the oldest represents a .3 increase in distribution scores, while the distance from the lowest occupational prestige to the

Table 5.17
Exposure/Personal Background Effect on Distribution Score

Year of Birth	Distribution Score	n
1912-1926	0.65	45
1927-1945	0.57	57
1946-1954	0.47	147
1955-1972	0.36*	27

Politically Influential Female Family Member	Distribution Score	n
NO	0.55	224
YES	0.40*	56

Education	Distribution Score	n
HIGH SCHOOL	0.44	101
COLLEGE	0.48	73
ADVANCED/PROFESSIONAL DEGREE	0.56	103

Occupational Prestige	Distribution Score	n
LOWEST	0.18	29
2	0.27	14
3	0.44	93
4	0.44	49
HIGHEST	0.68**	87

Ideology	Distribution Score	n
VERY LIBERAL	0.33	14
2	0.77	23
3	0.60	30
MODERATE	0.43	67
5	0.43	52
6	0.53	59
VERY CONSERVATIVE	0.55	32

**difference significant at $p < .01$
*difference significant at $p < .05$

Table 5.18
Multivariate Regression: Determinants of Distribution Score

	B	S.E
Outcome Dependency		
Competitiveness of District(-)	-.05	.08
Winnable Race(-)	-.02	.24
Accountability		
Tenure as Chair(-)	.01	.03
Recruiting Effort(-)	.01	.10
Cognitive Rigidity		
Confidence in Candidate Assessments(+)	.16**	.07
Discourage Unqualified Candidates(+)	.04	.04
Discourage Poor-Profile Candidates(+)	.13+	.09
Power over Outcome		
Recruiting Power(+)	.001	.26
Strength of Party Organization(+)	-.04	.05
Expect to Win Next Legislative Election(+)	.003	.24
Time Pressure		
Time to Evaluate Recruits(-)	-.12	.21
Exposure/Personal Background		
Age(-)	-.11*	.06
Family(-)	-.07	.10
Education(-)	.01	.06
Occupation(+)	.11**	.04
Ideology(+)	-.04	.03
Controls		
District Ideology(+)	.08*	.04
Party(?)	.04	.17
California(?)	-.02	.11
New Jersey(?)	-.08	.15
Ohio(?)	.06	.13
Party Chair Gender(?)	.22	.23
Constant	.57	.51

$R^2 = .20$
$N = 255$.

**p < .01
*p < .05
+p < .07

Note: The variables are coded as they were in the bivariate analysis, with the addition of gender (1 = male, 2 = female), party (1 = Republican, 2 = Democrat), and the dummy variables for the three states (with Tennessee being used as the default). Expected direction of relationship provided next to variable name.

highest represents a .4 increase. Meanwhile, for rigidity, higher confidence in candidate assessments corresponds to an increase of about .3 in distribution scores.

The widespread lack of success of the various theories outlined as potential predictors of perceptual bias in accounting for the distribution effect is perhaps due to the unusual nature of the distribution effect. The distribution effect does not represent self-generated bias as much as it represents bias generated against those whom society may be biased against. In other words, while party chairs display outgroup bias if they are uncomfortable with the outgroup, the distribution effect could occur regardless of the chair's personal feelings for different groups. As such, when a chair observes that a group is rare in politics, this scarcity could be attributed to many things, including not only the traits of the group but also the thought patterns of the electorate.

Given the nature of the distribution effect, then, it is both interesting and reasonable that the other variable that reaches statistical significance is district ideology. Party chairs in the most conservative districts have a distribution score .5 higher than those in the most liberal districts. While district ideology is apparently a significant component of distribution scores, it was not terribly relevant for outgroup scores, and this makes considerable sense. Again, the outgroup score is based on the dismissal of others because of one's own thinking, while the distribution score is based on the dismissal of others, not because of personal assessments, but because of societal patterns. Where conservatives are more prevalent (with the associated more "traditional" view of women's role [Bennett and Bennett 1992]), the prevalence of elected women and the societal view of the prevalence of elected women is more important. Note that personal ideology is not significant, indicating that it is not personal conservatism that inherently fosters bias but the perception of the conservative society that fosters distribution bias.

The distribution regression score results suggest the importance of rigidity, exposure, and district ideology in a model that, while not stunningly successful, is comparable to the levels of explained variance achieved in related work (Bennett and Bennett 1992). Thus, more political certainty, less exposure to diversity, and conservative districts appear to lead to greater attention to the prevalence of women in power and to the negative conclusions such attention typically fosters.

SUMMARY AND CONCLUSIONS

Bivariate results offered here allow easily observed comparisons to be made between the indicators and the outgroup and distribution scores, in a fashion similar to the presentation of most psychological research results. Meanwhile, the contribution of the two regression models is twofold. The success of the electoral competition measures in the outgroup score model and the success of district ideology in the distribution score model offer a means of distinguishing cases where the outgroup and distribution effects might be expected. Alternatively, the importance of exposure and rigidity in both models suggests the central role of these factors in determining one's proclivity toward perceptual bias.

Moreover, it should be noted that these models endeavor to expand upon typical procedures regarding the testing of hypotheses related to bias. Specifically, these models apply a number of complementary theories simultaneously instead of looking for effects in isolation from competing explanations. Further, these models utilize a variety of real-world indicators to apply findings largely born in the laboratory. Time distinctions here reflect real life, not seconds in a laboratory. Outcome dependency here exists in real political battles, not in receiving token inducements in an artificial setting. This is not meant to question the value of laboratory findings, but rather to emphasize that real world examination is the logical and necessary next step in testing the veracity and applicability of experimental results.

Perhaps the most obvious message contained in the analysis of the determinants of the outgroup and distribution effects is that there is a need for expansion and improvement in research on bias in the recruitment of women candidates. This study was conducted in a climate in which the dominant paradigm was that women did not face bias from recruiters. If women did not face bias, of course, there was no need to study the prevalence or determinants of different forms of bias. The results here should help provide a foundation for the assertion that women do face bias, and that such bias is of great enough significance to warrant the next generation of studies creating more focused research designs centered solely on exploring the determinants of the outgroup and distribution effects. This chapter represents an exploration of the determinants of bias, linking theory to real world political behavior. Future work can build on this to develop more and better political measures of the concepts, such as rigidity and exposure, that proved relevant here.

While Chapters 4 and 5 have endeavored to explore the prevalence of and determinants of two forms of bias, the effects of the outgroup and distribution effects have yet to be addressed. If there are relatively ubiquitous outgroup effects in party chair perceptions, especially among the more powerful, rigid, and least exposed, what are the consequences of this pattern for women candidates and for the electorate in general? This will be the focus of Chapter 6.

NOTES

1. Recall, in Figure 4.2, that lawyers were by the far the most prevalent occupation among legislative candidates.

2. Although this relationship and a few others are certainly significant, none of the relationships between the independent variables is strong enough to create collinearity problems (see Freund and Minton 1979).

3. Gender may have an interactive effect with other dependent variables that would not be apparent merely by including gender as an independent variable. In other words, if the determinants of outgroup bias were different for men and women, the current model would not reveal that. To examine this possibility, this model was modified to a version excluding women chairs and a version excluding men chairs. The dominant result is that the new models look quite similar to the original model, with most independent variables maintaining stable coefficients (especially in the women-excluded model). One variable that revealed noticeable change in the three models was the effect of discouraging poor-profile candidates. Discouraging poor-profile candidates, which is significant and positive in the original model, and in the men-excluded model, is not significant in the women-excluded model. Nevertheless, substantively important differences in the models were rare, suggesting that the determinants of outgroup bias are quite similar for men and women chairs.

6

The Effects of Bias

After examining the forms of perceptual bias and their determinants, the ultimate relevance of party chair bias remains in question until the effects of such bias are examined. That is to say, how many fewer women advance because of perceptual biases of the elite? One potential woman candidate commented, "The women who are active in our party by and large do not wish to hold public office. Perhaps because they have been discouraged from doing so."[1] The task addressed here, then, will be to assess the importance of elite bias or discouragement in comparison with other factors that affect women's candidacies. Toward that end, multivariate analyses of the determinants of women's legislative candidacies, operationalized first as the number of women on each chair's list of prospective candidates, then as whether a woman won the party's nomination for the legislature, will be presented. That will be followed by an interpretation of the regression results to estimate the ultimate effects of bias.

Another important potential by-product of bias, in addition to limiting the number of women who run, is limiting the types of women who run. Are different types of women candidates more susceptible to elite discouragement? Personality, ideology, and issue positions will be examined in order to assess whether women who are more likely to overcome elite treatment are notably different from women who are less likely to overcome it.

DETERMINANTS OF WOMEN'S CANDIDACIES

Because of the nature of this study, two different but quite relevant dependent variables can be utilized in assessing the determinants of women's candidacies. First, party chairs provided an estimate of the number of women being considered for a future run for the state house. Second, whether the county chair's party had a woman nominee for their state house legislative seat in the most recent election was determined from state election records. The advantage of using two measures is that they illuminate two different steps in the process and are derived from two different sources. The prospective candidate list is a map for the future drawn by the party chair, while the women nominees reflect the outcome of the candidate search independently reported. This negates fears that would exist if only the former were used as a dependent variable, such as the challenge that too much was being made of party chair perceptions as independent variable since the dependent variable is also a party chair perception, or that party chairs are not ultimately dominant in the choice of prospective candidates.

Unlike most research in this area, the unit of analysis will be the state legislative district rather than the entire state. In addition to being more practical given the data available here, some scholars point out that too much information is lost by aggregating district results to assess with a state unit of analysis (Werner 1993; Green 1995). Werner, in fact, argues that some determinants of women's candidacies, such as bias, disappear in aggregate data because such factors have only varying localized effects, not statewide effects.

Facilitating the assessment of the effects of elite bias are numerous studies that examine the prevalence of women legislators and its correlates. This previous research helps delineate the necessary controls to be used to more accurately assess the import of bias.

Party Situation

Democratic Party dominance has been found to be a significant predictor of women's candidacies. Interestingly, it has been labeled a significant negative factor (Rule 1990, 1981) as well as a significant positive factor (Matland and Brown 1992). The theory behind Rule's findings is that where the Democratic Party can win with any candidate, its nomination is more valuable and less likely to be shared with women. Further, the incentive to appease interested women would be limited due to the vast strength of the party.

Matland and Brown (1992) label Rule's conclusion a likely ecological fallacy created by assuming district-level events from state-level data. To wit, dominating a state on the statewide level is not equivalent to dominating all the districts within the state (Aistrup 1993). Typically, within even strong one-party states there are competitive districts and strong districts for both parties. Thus, the patterns that emerge on the district level may or may not correspond to the state level. Another problem with Democratic dominance as a negative factor is that typical (1970s-1980s) measures of party strength showed the Democrats to be dominant in the South. That again leaves one to wonder whether it was the Democratic Party that was impeding women or a spurious connection that ultimately illustrated only the South's effect on women's representation.

As mentioned, Matland and Brown (1992) find the Democratic Party to have a positive effect on women's candidacies. They theorize that the Democratic Party, because of its advantage in the gender gap and its greater commitment to issues of concern to women, is more interested in positioning itself as the party for women. Toward that end, Matland and Brown argue that the Democratic Party is more accommodating to the prospect of female candidacies.

Instead of blaming or crediting one of the national parties, Werner (1993) argues that it is the presence of a dominant party in the area, regardless of which party, that impedes women. Werner argues that where either party holds a dominant position, its incentives to attend to women as voters and as candidates are reduced. Further, where victory is assumed in the general election, there are more resources available to dedicate to shaping the primary field.

Party chairs were asked a variety of questions about their party and electoral situation. Since there is some dispute concerning the expected effects, measures utilized in the models tested here include the electoral strength and the organizational strength of the parties, as well as the specific effects of Democratic versus Republican dominance.

Electorate Attitudes

The mass-level opinion of women as candidates is considered by some to be a significant predictor of women's candidacies. Unfortunately, measures of public opinion on the legislative district level are not available. Typically, measures such as the electorate's education (Green 1995; Welch and Karnig 1975; Vandenbosch 1995), the electorate's income (Jones and Nelson 1981; Rule 1981), and social welfare commitments by government (Rule 1990) have been used as proxies for a more direct measure of public attitudes toward women candidates. These researchers have found that higher education, higher income, and higher social welfare commitments are positively correlated with the number of women legislators.

Werner has taken this method one step further by attempting to estimate public opinion with regard to "egalitarian attitudes." Egalitarian attitudes, operationalized by Werner, simply reflect whether a person is comfortable with the notion of women as political leaders. Werner's measure allows one to simulate the level of egalitarian attitudes by first estimating the relationship between demographic variables and egalitarian responses in a national survey and then weighting demographic data from legislative districts to produce an egalitarian score for each district (see also Jackson and King 1989; Erikson 1978). Werner does not conclude that every gradation of opinion has great influence on women candidates. Instead, Werner finds that those in the least egalitarian districts are significantly less supportive of women candidates. Thus, examined on the aggregate level, women do not suffer at the hands of biased voters. However, in certain districts where attitudes are particularly negative, women may be adversely affected by mass opinion.

Werner's measure is adapted to provide an estimate of egalitarian attitudes in each district. In keeping with Werner's findings, the score represents a dichotomous distinction between districts scoring in the bottom 10% and all other districts.

Women's Activity

In an effort to capture a sense of how much interest and ability women have to serve in legislative office, scholars have turned to various demographic indicators. Women in the labor force (Rule 1990; Hill 1981), amount of education among women (Jones and Nelson 1981), the number of women in professional occupations (Rule 1990), and the number of women's groups (Rule 1990) have all been found to be positively related to the number of women legislators.

In theory, interest and ability should be precursors to women's political activity, which then facilitates women's candidacies. A more direct measure of women's activity, the percentage of party activists who are female, could be used to incorporate these factors while perhaps forging a stronger political connection with the resulting behavior of women.

Party chairs were asked to estimate the percentage of female activists in their county party. Party chairs, of course, could offer a self-serving response when asked how many party activists are women. They might, for example, exaggerate the number in order to make their party appear more inclusive. In order to address this problem, both party chairs and potential women candidates were asked their assessments of women's party activity. This allows a comparison and correction to be made if needed.

Party chairs who responded that women made up less than 50% of county party activists tended to correspond rather closely to the estimates offered by women potential candidates from the same county. Meanwhile, party chairs who responded that women made up 50% or more of the activists in their party were giving responses that averaged 14 points higher than women offering assessments of the same county party. For those over 50%, then, the party chairs' estimates were reduced by half the difference with the potential women candidates' estimates.[2]

Political Culture

Political culture, variously operationalized, has been found to be a quite important determinant of women's candidacies (Rule 1990; Hill 1981; Jones and Nelson 1981; Green 1995; Vandenbosch 1995; Werner 1993). As indicators of political culture, these researchers have used Elazar's typology (1984), and Sharkansky's adaptation of Elazar's work (1969), as well as more concrete measures of this abstract concept such as whether the state had suffrage before 1920, the number of women in office previously, and the number of Christians in the state's voting population. Regardless of how it is operationalized, the thrust of this work indicates that a tradition, atmosphere, or culture that has encouraged women's activity in the past encourages women's candidacies in the present.[3]

Given that this is an examination of district-level data, instead of statewide data, most of the indicators of political culture are not very useful since they provide only statewide variation. The best remaining indicator of district culture, then, is the history of the district regarding the election of women. Here, election of a woman to the state legislature in any term during the 1970s is treated as evidence of a more conducive political culture.[4]

State Effects

Various attributes of individual states and their legislatures have been hypothesized to be important in the process of electing women. Specifically, multi-member districts (Rule 1990; Vandenbosch 1995), lower legislative compensation (Hill 1981), and smaller constituency size (Hill 1981; Matland and Brown 1992) have been associated with more women legislators. The predominant conclusion is that factors such as these create or alleviate bias against women in state legislative races. Werner (1993), however, argues that nothing inherent in legislative compensation or professionalism fosters bias. Instead, any effect these variables have is on the incentive for the elite to act on bias that already exists. Ultimately, Werner finds that professionalism of state legislatures does not have a significant effect on women's candidacies.

Given the questions about their significance and the level of measurement utilized here, the effects of distinctive state legislative forms will be accounted for with dummy variables for the states studied. The four states were chosen to provide a diversity of features with regard to their state legislatures, providing the possibility of interesting contrasts between the states (see Table 3.1). While this method does not allow one to isolate the effects of, for example, legislator compensation, this method does allow for major effects of state differences to be accounted for and provides a further control when testing the significance of bias.

Elite Bias Measures

Bias measures will be based on the scores developed in the last chapter. Specifically, the outgroup measure is an interaction between the outgroup score and party chair gender, while the distribution measure is an interaction between the distribution score and the number of women legislators elected in the party chair's state. Including these interactions allows a distinction to be made between cases where outgroup effect will hurt women (where male chairs are outgroup biased) and cases where it would not (when women chairs are outgroup biased), and between cases where the distribution effect would be expected to hurt women (where women officeholders are rare) and cases where it would not (where women officeholders are comparatively prevalent). Details of the operationalization of the two interactions are available in Tables 6.1 and 6.2.

In addition, there is reason to suspect that bias might have different effects in "longshot districts." Diamond (1977), Carroll and Strimling (1983), and Werner (1993) find disproportionately large numbers of women running against well-established incumbents. An interaction was therefore created between the outgroup score and electoral longshot status to determine if increasing the number of women running in the worst districts is another ramification of bias (see Table 6.3).[5]

Table 6.1
Outgroup Interaction Operationalization

Outgroup Interaction Score Used in Model	Outgroup Score	Gender of Chair	Expected Effect
-2	2	Women	Very Pro-Female Candidates
-1	1	Women	Pro-Female Candidates
0	0	Women and Men	Neutral
1	1	Men	Pro-Male Candidates
2	2	Men	Very Pro-Male Candidates

Table 6.2
Distribution Interaction Operationalization

Distribution Interaction Score Used in Model	Distribution Score	Distribution of Women Officeholders[a]	Expected Effect
-2	2	High	Very Pro-Female Candidates
-1	1	High	Pro-Female Candidates
0	0	All	Neutral
1	1	Low	Pro-Male Candidates
2	2	Low	Very Pro-Male Candidates

[a]Distinguished by adding number of women elected in each state and each chairs' county. The high category is above the mean, the low category below the mean.

Table 6.3
Bias/Longshot Interaction Operationalization

Bias/Longshot Interaction Score Used in Model	Outgroup Interaction Score	Longshot District[a]	Expected Effect
-1	1,2	no	Fewer Female Candidates
0	0,-1,-2	either	Middle
1	1,2	yes	More Female Candidates

[a]Based on chair's assessment of party's likelihood of winning.

Table 6.4
Multivariate Regression: Determinants of Women's Prospective Candidacies

	B	S.E
Elite Bias		
Outgroup Score(-)	-.40**	.12
Distribution Score(-)	-.25+	.17
Bias/Longshot Race(+)	.10+	.06
Women		
Women Party Activity(+)	.08*	.04
Mass Behavior		
Non-Egalitarian Attitudes(-)	-.48**	.16
Political Culture(+)	.65**	.11
Party Dominance		
Party(?)	.09	.13
Strength of Party Organization(-)	.07	.06
Electoral Competitiveness(-)	.24	.31
State Variation		
California(?)	.28	.24
New Jersey(?)	-.09	.26
Ohio(?)	.03	.19
constant	1.23	.74

$R^2 = .46$

N = 255.

**p < .01
*p < .05
+p < .07

Note: The variables and their coding are described in the text, with the exception of party (1 = Republican, 2 = Democratic) and the dummy variables for the three states (with Tennessee being used as the default). Expected direction of relationship provided next to variable name.

Prospective Women Candidate Results

Table 6.4 provides the regression results for the number of prospective women candidates. Specifically, the dependent variable used here is the number of women in the party chair's list of the top five prospective state legislative candidates. Negative coefficients, then, indicate measures associated with fewer women candidates, and positive coefficients indicate measures associated with more women candidates.

Table 6.4 indicates that bias is indeed a significant factor in determining the number of prospective women candidates. The outgroup effect plays a more significant role than does the distribution effect, but both forms display the expected relationship. The outgroup measure results in a coefficient of -.40, statistically significant at p < .01. Applying the coefficients while holding all else constant reveals that the expected number of women candidates varies from 3.0 out of 5.0 for outgroup-biased women party chairs, to 2.2 for unbiased male and female party chairs, to 1.4 for outgroup-biased male party chairs. In other words, outgroup-biased male party chairs have almost one less woman on their list than do the unbiased chairs. This progression, which will be discussed further in a subsequent section, is obviously alarming for the prospects of women because there are far more male party chairs (and outgroup-biased male party chairs) than female party chairs.

The distribution score meanwhile has a coefficient of -.25, statistically significant at p < .07. Applying the coefficient for the distribution score suggests that distribution-biased party chairs in low prevalence areas have .5 fewer women on their list of five prospective candidates than do the unbiased.

In short, the personal perceptual biases of party chairs have a clear and significant effect on the number of prospective women candidates the chair is considering. This is the case even as the model controls for the activity of women, the attitudes of the electorate, political culture, and other factors hypothesized by scholars to affect the number of women candidates.

The exception to this pattern exists where party leaders are biased and they fully expect their party to lose. Here, outgroup-biased male party chairs have slightly more women in mind for a future legislative race than do biased party chairs in other situations. According to these results, biased party chairs in longshot races do tend to seek sacrificial women to fill the ballot, where they otherwise might encourage men if a better electoral situation existed.

Turning to the other variables, not surprisingly, women's activity in the party contributes to the number of prospective women candidates. According to the model, for every 12% increase in the number of women party activists there is an increase of one woman on the list of prospective candidates. Obviously, there must be a reservoir of women's activity and interest for women candidates to emerge, and this suggests that added activity is indeed rewarded.

Could party chairs or biased party chairs manipulate the number of women activists as a means to hinder women? While possible, this scenario does not seem very likely because party chairs need women activists for their exploitable labor (Margolis 1980; Sapiro and Farah 1980; Costantini and Craik 1972; Clark, Hadley, and Darcy 1989). Moreover, the thrust of potential women candidate survey responses certainly does not indicate that these women have witnessed women being discouraged from giving time and effort on behalf of their party, especially when menial tasks must be performed.

Mass attitudes also contribute to women's candidacies. The districts with the least egalitarian attitudes appear to have .5 fewer women on the prospective candidate list than do other districts. Since women's activity and elite bias are separately accounted for (and since there is no strong collinearity; see Appendix D), this is an independent effect of the electorate on the pre-candidacy process. Because of the nature of this data, one can test and find that it is not merely by directly limiting women's inclination for political activity that mass attitudes matter. Nor is it merely by influencing elite attitudes toward women that mass attitudes have an effect. Previous efforts in this area have been limited because they lacked independent measures of elite attitudes (Werner 1993; Darcy, Welch, and Clark 1994). Ultimately, they could only infer elite attitudes and behavior from electoral results. In the process, one could not distinguish between elite attitudes and elites attempting to follow mass attitudes. Thus, it is not entirely a conventional finding to assert that anti-egalitarian mass attitudes create their own independent barrier to women's candidacies, presumably by reducing the incentive for all actors involved to pursue women candidates.

To this point, elite, women, and mass factors have all proven relevant to women's candidacies. The fourth significant determinant is political culture. As previously argued, political culture is a larger atmosphere that affects all participants in the process. Favorable political culture, here operationalized as having elected a woman legislator in the 1970s, corresponds to an added .65 women candidates.

Elazar defined political culture as the "habits, perspectives, and attitudes that influence political life" (1984, 110). While there may be better indicators of the intangible political culture of a district, using the history of elected women legislators taps the most relevant aspects (Rule 1990). Thus, the districts' habits and perspectives regarding elected women contribute to women's candidacies (see also MacManus 1981), in addition to the specific effects of elite, mass, and women's behavior.

Thus, in a model whose predictive success ($R^2 = .46$) is comparable to similar efforts, and using appropriate controls, the clear finding is that elite bias matters.

Nominations of Women Results

Interestingly, Table 6.5 provides a very similar picture when whether a woman wins the party's legislative seat nomination in the district is the dependent variable. Because the dependent variable is dichotomous, a logistic regression model is used. Again, culture, women's activity, mass attitudes, and bias play important roles.

Interpreting logistic regression results is most easily accomplished by adapting the odds ratio. The third column in Table 6.5 contains the odds ratio converted into a percentage for each statistically significant variable. The resulting number is the percentage change in the likelihood of the dependent variable changing values associated with each unit of the independent variable.

The effect of women's party activity, for example, is estimated as increasing the likelihood of a woman winning the nomination by 1% for every unit change in women's party activity. A change from the bottom of the range to the top on

Table 6.5
Logistic Regression: Determinants of Women's Nominations

	B	S.E	Odds Ratio %
Elite Bias			
Outgroup Score(-)	-.38*	.21	-46
Distribution Score(-)	-.24*	.15	-30
Bias/Longshot Race(+)	.10*	.06	12
Women			
Women Party Activity(+)	.09**	.02	1
Mass Behavior			
Non-Egalitarian Attitudes(-)	-.50*	.29	-39
Political Culture(+)	.69*	.36	100
Party Dominance			
Party(?)	-.10	.15	
Strength of Party Organization(-)	-.24	.27	
Electoral Competitiveness(-)	.31	.27	
State Variation			
California(?)	.02	.99	
New Jersey(?)	-.61	.69	
Ohio(?)	.08	.30	
constant	-.14	.44	

percent correct 92
Chi-square   113.2
probability   <.0001
N   255.

**p < .01
*p < .05
+p < .07

Note: The variables and their coding are described in the text, with the exception of party (1 = Republican, 2 = Democratic) and the dummy variables for the three states (with Tennessee being used as the default). Expected direction of relationship provided next to variable name.

women's party activity produces a 55% increase in the likelihood of a woman winning the nomination for the legislative seat.

Districts with the least egalitarian mass attitudes are estimated to have a 39% lower chance of electing a woman legislator. Meanwhile, districts with favorable political culture are twice as likely to have a woman legislative nominee.

Again, the outgroup bias interaction plays an important role, while the distribution score has a somewhat smaller impact. Outgroup-biased male party chairs have an estimated 92% lower chance of having a woman win the nomination in their district than do unbiased men and women chairs. Distribution-biased chairs with few women officeholders are 60% less likely to have a female win the nomination than are chairs with no distribution bias.

The ramifications of bias are quite different in longshot districts. Here, again, biased male party chairs are more likely to have a female nominee than are biased chairs in other situations (by approximately 24%). Toward that end, a few potential women candidates offered some variation of this New Jersey Democrat's comments, "I was encouraged to run once, when no one, I mean no one, wanted the race." Bias thus affects women by discouraging their candidacies generally and discouraging their opportunity for success by channelling them into longshot races.

In a model that correctly predicts 92% of the cases (which is a significant improvement over simply guessing the majority position each time, and an improvement over related work [see Green 1995]), with powerful controls representing the activity of women, mass attitudes, and political culture, bias is a significant impediment to women in securing legislative seat nominations. These results strongly suggest that to ignore elite perceptions is to not only ignore an important factor, it also serves to minimize the difficulty prospective women candidates face in seeking office.

Among the variables that did not have a significant effect in either model were party and ideology. Previous research offers support for a variety of expectations, including either party as a negative force. However, finding little effect is consistent with some recent work arguing that both parties have the same incentives and disincentives to pursue women candidates (Carroll 1994; Delli Carpini and Fuchs 1993).

Competitiveness of the districts also failed to directly influence the number of women candidates or the likelihood of a woman nominee. However, considered more broadly, competitiveness is very relevant. In addition to the effects evident in the longshot/bias interaction, recall the important connection between competitiveness and bias found in Chapter 5 (for example, Table 5.11), where greater competitiveness was associated with less bias. While the findings here indicate that competitiveness does not have a strong direct effect, competitiveness is nevertheless an important factor through its influence on the amount of bias. To wit, more competitive districts discourage bias, while less competitive districts allow anti-women bias to fester. In the process, since we are more likely to find bias in less competitive districts, we are more likely to find women being weeded out from active candidacy or being channeled into hopeless races in the less competitive districts.[6]

Another component that does not directly influence women's candidacies is the structural variations between the states. Again, while this finding is not consistent with many previous studies, it is consistent with Werner's (1993) conclusion that the process that determines women's candidacies is an individual-level process, with individual attitudes, not state rules and institutions, playing the dominant role (see also Darcy, Welch, and Clark 1994). Previous research may have exaggerated the importance of state structure when it ignored individual attitudes.

That the same factors (elite bias, women's party activity, political culture, and egalitarian attitudes) are significant in the two models offers strong support for the conclusion that these variables are truly important. Moreover, this consistency

Table 6.6
Predicted Number of Women Candidates by Outgroup Category

Party Chair

Outgroup Interaction Category	*Women Candidates*[a]
High Outgroup Biased Women(-2)	3.0
Low Outgroup Biased Women(-1)	2.6
Unbiased Men and Women(0)	2.2
Low Outgroup Biased Men(1)	1.8
High Outgroup Biased Men(2)	1.4

[a]Number of women out of five potential candidates chair is considering for a future state legislative race, calculated from multivariate regression coefficient.

suggests that the importance of elites in the process should not be minimized. With respect to gender, factors that influence elites' creation of prospective candidate lists also affect the eventual nomination outcome.

The clear and consistent finding that emerges from these two models is that elite bias matters. These models indicate that elite bias results in fewer prospective women candidates and fewer women nominees, except where party chairs see their chances for victory to be quite remote, in which case bias is associated with encouraging women's ill-fated candidacies.

BIAS AND THE NUMBER OF WOMEN CANDIDATES

While the coefficients in both models are statistically significant, ultimately, applying the estimates in the models shows that the effect of the distribution bias is not dramatically negative. This is due to the infrequency with which party chairs fit that description (see Table 5.1).

Conversely, considering the prevalence of outgroup bias only magnifies its importance. The coefficient in the first model and the odds ratio in the second indicate the important differences produced as one moves from outgroup-biased male party chairs, to unbiased party chairs, to outgroup-biased female party chairs. This, combined with knowledge of the prevalence of each category, offers perhaps the best estimate of the effect of outgroup bias.

Consider the estimated number of women candidates predicted for each outgroup category (presented in Table 6.6). The net effect of outgroup bias is not clear with this information alone. If, for example, there were equal numbers of cases in each category, the result would be equivalent to having no bias at all since the negative effect of male outgroup bias on women would be negated by the positive effect of female outgroup bias. In other words, the ultimate effect of outgroup bias on the number of women candidates would be nil. This, however, is not the case.

Table 6.7
Proportion of Sample in Each Outgroup Category

Party Chair

Outgroup Interaction Category	*Proportion*
High Outgroup-Based Women(-2)	8%
Low Outgroup-Biased Women(-1)	5%
Unbiased Men and Women(0)	14%
Low Outgroup-Biased Men(1)	28%
High Outgroup-Biased Men(2)	45%

N = 280.

The percentage of the sample that fits in each outgroup interaction category is depicted in Table 6.7. The breakdown provided in Table 6.7 shows that there are almost six times as many male party chairs in the high outgroup category as there are female party chairs who fit that description. Multiplying the predicted number of women candidates by the proportionate size of the category and summing the results reveals that outgroup bias, in the proportions it exists, reduces the number of prospective women candidates from 2.2 out of 5 to 1.8 out of 5. Alternatively, in terms of the 280 party chairs who listed 1,400 prospective legislative candidates, this effect may be considered as reducing the number of women from 616 to 504.

Applying the same procedure to the women nominees, Table 6.8 provides the predicted likelihood of a woman nominee in each outgroup category. Again, using those results with the relative size of each category reveals that absence of bias is associated with a 33% likelihood of a woman nominee, while the ultimate effect of outgroup bias results in a 23% likelihood of a woman nominee. In terms of the 280 districts in the sample, outgroup bias reduces women from 92 nominations to 64 nominations.

No matter how it is presented, outgroup bias has a significant effect that quite obviously harms potential women candidates. In a larger sense, this process constricts the choices of the electorate, affects our representation, and removes potential role models from the eyes of younger citizens.

One could object, however, and argue that both models presented focus on women's candidacies and not women officeholders, and that perhaps the determinants of women winning office are not assessed. However, there are two important mitigating factors that reduce the significance of this problem. First, there are numerous studies that conclude that women who secure nominations are as likely to succeed as men in similar situations (see Chapter 2). Ergo, factors that determine women's candidacy rate are the factors that determine how many women win office.

Table 6.8
Predicted Likelihood of Women Nominees by Outgroup Category

Party Chair

Outgroup Interaction Category	*Women Nominees*[a]
High Outgroup-Biased Women(-2)	55%
Low Outgroup-Biased Women(-1)	44%
Unbiased Men and Women(0)	33%
Low Outgroup-Biased Men(1)	22%
High Outgroup-Biased Men(2)	11%

[a]Likelihood that party chair's legislative district had a woman nominee for the state legislature, calculated from logistic regression odds ratio.

Second, it should be again noted that there is a key distinction between this work and previous research that has focused on the treatment of the nominees. When studying the treatment of nominees, scholars have failed to find evidence of bias (Darcy, Welch, and Clark 1994; Burrell 1994a; McLean 1994). This is a common finding and a sensible one given that parties are not inclined to thwart their only hope of winning by hurting their nominees. Thus, previous research suggests that the nominees produced by the system will compete on a relatively level playing field in terms of elite treatment. However, the argument here and the evidence here is that who becomes the nominee is affected by bias, thus making candidacy the appropriate dependent variable.

THE WOMEN WHO EMERGE

While bias is found to affect the number of prospective women candidates, the number of nominees, and the types of races they are encouraged to pursue, there is another significant potential residue of bias. In addition to limitations on the number of women who participate as candidates, elite bias could also influence the types of women who participate. Browning (1968) and Kirkpatrick (1974) both note the vast potential differences between those who are capable of advancing their political fortunes essentially by themselves and those who are reliant on encouragement from others.

The importance of this question is that it represents one indication of the ramifications of party recruiting power. Specifically, if party chairs exhibit any reluctance to support women candidates, as the evidence here indicates, then to find women candidates is to find women who are willing to run without support (i.e., self-starters). If the women self-starters are significantly different from the other women in some dimension of political behavior, then the elites could be shaping the output of political women by failing to pursue women dependent on encouragement and leaving us disproportionately represented by self-starters. The differences between self-starters and those who need to be recruited have not been extensively explored, thus the scope of possible personality, ideology, and issue differences is unknown.

Are there significant differences between women self-starters and those who are not? This question can be assessed by asking the potential women candidates about the likelihood of them running under three different conditions: "being recruited by your party to run for state legislature," "not being recruited by your party," and "being discouraged from running by your party." With this question a measure of willingness to be a self-starter was created, which can then be used in conjunction with a series of trait descriptions and issue positions to determine if self-starters are different. Three groups were created. Self-starters are those who replied that there was a greater than 50% chance of their running for the state legislature even if they were being discouraged by their party. Reluctants are those who indicated there was a greater than 50% chance of their running only if they were being recruited. The middle category consists of the irresolute group, those who stated there was a greater than 50% chance of their running even if they were not being recruited, but not if they are being discouraged from running. Of those who expressed interest in running, 49% could be labeled reluctants, 32% irresolutes, and 19% self-starters.

At the most basic level, these numbers provide another indication that recruiting matters. There is a substantial reduction in the number of willing women candidates as party enthusiasm is replaced first with apathy and then with hostility. Although not involving complicated regression analyses or the application of those results, these simple data reinforce the finding derived from the party chairs; both sources support the conclusion that there will be dramatically fewer women candidates when elites are unreceptive.

Beyond the shrinking size of these groups, their makeup is the concern. The potential women candidates were asked to provide their ideology on a seven-point scale (1 = very liberal, 7 = very conservative.) At first glance, the three groups appear quite similar with regard to ideology, suggesting there might not be a difference associated with propensity to run. As revealed in Table 6.9, however, when party is controlled for, a different result appears. Among Democrats, self-starters are the most liberal group, while among Republicans, self-starters are the most conservative. This pattern suggests that reluctance on the part of party chairs to support women may result in somewhat more ideological, less moderate characteristics in the women who persevere in pursuing elected office.

This interesting pattern with regard to ideology leads one to wonder if these three groups are distinctive with regard to issues, specifically issues of direct relevance to women. The potential women candidates were asked to give their position on a seven-point scale (1 = not desirable, 7 = very desirable) on three issues: the Equal Rights Amendment, more strict enforcement of sexual harassment, and affirmative action programs to benefit women. Surprisingly, given the previous results, no clear pattern develops with regard to these three issues (Table 6.10). For the most part the patterns are inconsistent and do not show the

Table 6.9
Ideology by Proclivity to Run for the Legislature

Democrats

Proclivity to Run[a]	Ideology[b]
Reluctant	3.6
Irresolute	3.4
Self-Starter	3.3**

Republicans

Proclivity to Run[a]	Ideology[b]
Reluctant	4.5
Irresolute	4.6
Self-Starter	4.8**

N = 219.

**difference significant at p < .01
[a]measurement described in text.
[b]measurement on seven point scale (1 = very liberal, 7 = very conservative).

Table 6.10
Issue Positions by Proclivity to Run for the Legislature

Democrats

Proclivity to Run[a]	ERA[b]	Harassment	Affirmative Action
Reluctant	5.9	6.1	5.7
Irresolute	6.6	5.9	5.8
Self Starter	6.1	6.0	5.6

Republicans

Proclivity to Run	ERA	Harassment	Affirmative Action
Reluctant	5.2	5.0	4.2
Irresolute	5.4	5.0	4.3
Self Starter	5.3	4.8	4.0

N = 215.

[a]measurement described in text.
[b]issue positions describe response to seven point scale (1 = not desirable, 7 = very desirable) regarding passage of the ERA, more strict enforcement of sexual harassment, and affirmative action programs to benefit women.

Table 6.11
Gender Personality Trait Scale by Proclivity to Run for the Legislature

Proclivity to Run[a]	_Gender Trait Scale_[b]
Reluctant	3.1
Irresolute	2.8
Self Starter	1.0**

N = 216.

**difference significant at $p < .01$
[a]measurement described in text.
[b]lower score indicates more typically male traits (measurement described in text).

tendency for the slightly more radical positions among self-starters that appeared on the ideology measure.

On the surface this pattern does not make very much sense. Self-starters, who are more ideologically extreme, are not more extreme with regard to the issues of central importance to women. The personality trait responses might explain this situation, however.

Potential women candidates were asked to rate themselves on the personality traits introduced in Chapter 4 on a seven-point scale: 1 = very characteristic, 7 = not characteristic. The 15 traits included five typically associated with men, five typically associated with women, and five typically neutral traits. A gender index was then created by subtracting each respondent's average score on the "female traits" from their average score on the "male traits." The gender index could potentially range from -6 to 6, with higher scores indicating greater association with the "female traits" and lower scores indicating greater association with "male traits." The gender index results indicate that self-starters are more likely to describe themselves with the typically male traits than either irresolutes and reluctants, while reluctants are more likely to describe themselves with the typically female traits than the other two groups (Table 6.11).

Potential women candidates were also asked to report how important it is for their party to win the "women's vote," on a five-point scale (1 = not important, 5 = very important). Consistent with the personality finding, self-starters report placing less value on the women's vote than do the other groups (Table 6.12).

These results indicate that a greater association with women may make women less likely to overcome party bias. Thus, the women who are most likely to overcome party obstacles are somewhat more radical, but if anything, less connected with women. This is important, as some have argued that gender

Table 6.12
Importance of Women's Vote by Proclivity to Run for the Legislature

	Importance of
Proclivity to Run[a]	*Women's Vote*[b]
Reluctant	4.6
Irresolute	4.4
Self Starter	4.2**

N = 219.

**difference significant at p < .01
[a]measurement described in text.
[b]closer to 5 indicates greater importance of women's vote (measurement described in text).

connections significantly influence the work of government (Stivers 1993). Women legislators, according to Rosenthal (1996), tend to govern in a more inclusive fashion, emphasizing discussion over domination. However, she finds that in some settings women legislators can become more stereotypically "male" than male legislators. Clearly, if bias makes party leaders less likely to recruit women, then the women who persevere are disproportionately those who did not need to be recruited. These results suggest that those women are distinctive--specifically, more radical and less connected with women. These self-starters may be less capable of providing a different perspective from their male colleagues, and according to Rosenthal, may be less likely to contribute to consensual governing.

SUMMARY AND CONCLUSIONS

Examining the determinants of women's legislative candidacies shows that women's political activity, inegalitarian mass attitudes, political culture, and elite bias are key factors. The finding that elite bias hurts women is an important departure from the conventional wisdom as, in this analysis, both the outgroup effect and the distribution effect are associated with a reduction in the number of women prospective candidates and women nominees. The outgroup effect, however, as further analysis reveals, has the more substantial effect, with estimates showing it reducing women's candidacies by up to one-third in comparison to what would be expected with no bias. In longshot districts, where women presumably have little or no chance of success, this pattern is reversed, as bias is associated with slightly more women candidates.

The independent variables (women's political activity, inegalitarian mass attitudes, political culture, and elite bias) that are significant in a model predicting the number of prospective women candidates are also significant in a model predicting the likelihood of a woman nominee. This consistency serves to increase confidence in the centrality of these factors in the women's candidacy equation.

While outgroup bias is found to have a great effect on the number of women candidates, failure to encourage prospective women candidates is found to have another significant effect. To the extent women are going to overcome bias against them from party leaders, they must have the interest and capability to run on their own, as self-starters. These self-starters, however, are not representative of women potential candidates. They are more ideological and less connected to women in that self-starters describe themselves as being less focused on the importance of the women's vote, while having more typically male traits.

The bias of leaders, then, has three substantively important but separate effects. These three major findings can be summarized in one analogy: Outgroup bias keeps a significant number of women out of the choir, puts women in places where they cannot be heard, while in the process those that can overcome the conductor's skepticism are more likely to mimic the baritone than to sing lead soprano.

NOTES

1. Tennessee Democrat.

2. Where there was no corresponding woman candidate to make a comparison, half the overall mean difference (7) was removed from the party chair's estimate.

3. While most of the factors discussed here have obvious links to either voters, elites, or women, the nexus of political culture is hard to specify. In general, most researchers believe all three groups are affected, as voters and elites become more accepting and women more willing to participate in areas with favorable political culture. This lack of specificity is useful in some respects as the models used here have separate measures that clearly reflect elite bias, mass attitudes, and the activity of women, allowing us to view these groups separately, while culture facilitates an assessment of the atmosphere collectively.

4. All terms in the 1970s are considered, rather than any more recent years, in order to lessen the complication of having the same woman occupy the seat during the past and current terms, thereby clouding the effects of political culture with such things as incumbency advantage. Comparison was made on a county-by-county basis since district lines typically changed over the period.

5. Only the outgroup score is utilized in the interaction, and not the distribution score, because there is too little variance in the distribution scores to create a meaningful interaction.

6. While the connection between competitiveness and bias is important, it is not at all strong here (shown in Appendix D) because of the coding for the interaction between gender of chair and bias, which was meant to draw a distinction between the likely effects of outgroup bias for women and men party chairs.

7

Conclusion

From the first data presented, this research has developed evidence that significant bias against women candidates exists, and that this bias from party leaders has significant consequences. How is this bias communicated? For some, as is made obvious in Chapter 4, bias is communicated in the baldest and most inescapable ways. However, for most women, such blatant examples are the exception. To wit, one woman candidate commented on the imbalance in treatment men and women receive from her party's leaders, "Some are groomed to become big, some are not, but it's not like they announce it on a billboard."[1] What does occur with quite disturbing regularity, according to this and other potential women candidates, is more subtle but no less significant than the hateful words some have heard.

Many of these potential women candidates refer to "latent" preferences for men and male candidates that they have observed. In their experiences, party leaders may not explicitly voice their preferences, but instead communicate quietly through word and deed that male candidates are sought and women are not. That is, women are discouraged, "not in an overt fashion, but the party covertly favors men."[2]

Lack of information and inclusion were frequently cited by women as the mechanisms by which the preference for male candidates was experienced. Women find, "men in the party do not share concerns with women as they do with other men,"[3] or that "the good old boys exclude women from serious side talks on strategy."[4] As one woman put it, "There is a communication breakdown for various reasons . . . including men have more opportunities to discuss (i.e., coffee at restaurants, 'chance meetings.')"[5]

The last comment suggests one source of this information imbalance is the choice of setting for political discussion. Not only do "male counterparts meet with other males on issues but rarely with women,"[6] but they partake in such meetings in places where women are either unwelcome or uncomfortable. One woman noted that in her party, "Males held meetings in bars or on the golf course (I did not go to these places)."[7] This pattern results, according to another woman, in a "Locker room/golf buddy disadvantage"[8] for women activists.

Even when women are included in political events, they often feel less welcome than their male counterparts. One woman noted, "I'm ignored at some political functions while the leaders talk to men,"[9] while others noted the tendency for less effort to be made to introduce women to the leaders at party functions.

At meetings, and other party events, women often report a difference in atmosphere (compared to the reaction to men) when they do assert themselves and offer their ideas. Some women recount being met with persistent dull stares, while men are more apt to be listened to with rapt attention. In the words of one woman, "it is hard to be recognized in this atmosphere--even to participate in discussions,"[10] while another added that, to her party, "it appears I don't exist."[11] In the reaction to their ideas about politics, these women frequently report that encouragement and words of praise are hard to come by. To wit, one woman commented, "I often feel my comments, if offered by a man, would be approved of."[12] To the extent their ideas are utilized, it is often the case that credit has been coopted by a man in the party. "In group discussions, if a man makes the same point that a woman does, he receives more credit and attention for it," was a typical comment.[13]

In the process, many women come to feel less valued than men in their party. Even though they may not have certifiable proof or been dismissed with a memorable quote, the majority of the potential women candidates feel that bias affects the party process in a way detrimental to women. One woman's comment typifies the mundane but ubiquitous treatment women receive in party settings: "Throughout my political experience, there have always been various degrees of overlooking the women's opinion to hear what a man has to say. So ordinary, no one really notices."[14]

Zepatos and Kaufman (1995, 146) sound themes quite similar to those expressed by the women candidates when they conclude,

The old boy's network doesn't have a listing in the phone book, an office, or official club meetings. The network exits in men's clubs, in board rooms and on the golf course. Men have used business, social, and political contacts for years for a variety of purposes. Networks are based on the simple principle that through sharing information, each person in the network gains more power.

The nature of these women's comments helps illustrate the thrust of the findings reported here. Rather than augmenting the conclusion that women do not suffer bias from political elites to the status of conventional wisdom, this research suggests that women are subject to bias from party leaders. Not a "male conspiracy," but simple and significant perceptual bias, most notably in the form of the outgroup effect. Male party leaders, who are in the vast majority, consistently express preferences for candidates who are more like themselves. This requires neither secret society meetings nor even conscious decisions. Instead, both the pattern of responses from party leaders and the experiences related by potential women candidates suggest that party chairs, left to their own devices to make a subjective evaluation, are prone to rely on bias in helping to sort prospective and potential candidates.

The large discrepancy in this conclusion from that of other researchers owes in large part to the evidence utilized. By relying exclusively on the treatment of nominated women, previous studies restricted their sample to disproportionately successful women. By ignoring the attitudes of party leaders, these researchers were forced to infer attitudes, again from the treatment of nominated candidates. Ultimately, in failing to directly assess the attitudes and behaviors of the relevant participants, previous research minimized the possibility of witnessing bias, thus compromising conclusions that bias does not exist. This research relied on direct responses from party chairs and potential women candidates. As a result, the potential range of success on the part of these women candidates provides a more realistic set of experiences of which to enquire. At the same time, allowing the actors involved to express their own attitudes reduces the noise inherent in inferring attitudes from electoral results, in the process creating a more precise measurement of the matter at hand.

SUMMARY OF FINDINGS

The results of this study indicate that the interaction between party chairs and potential women candidates is affected by bias. Such bias has a deleterious effect on the recruitment of women. As a starting point, a majority of potential women candidates indicated that they had witnessed discriminatory treatment against women in their parties.

The possible existence of the outgroup effect and the distribution effect, two forms of bias that might explain this biased treatment of women, were investigated. The fundamental difference between the outgroup and distribution effects is simply the origin of negative presumptions. The outgroup effect theory posits that assumptions of similar beliefs and positive initial evaluations are fostered by surface similarity with the evaluator, while those who are outwardly dissimilar are treated as members of a homogenous and less-esteemed group. The distribution effect, on the other hand, does not hinge on estimates of similarity with the evaluator. Instead, the distribution effect is derived from essentially statistical conclusions that certain types of people are more likely to hold high-status positions. In other words, the differential distribution of men and women into distinct productive roles feeds the creation of gender-based assessments. Thus, because women are more likely to pursue home-based or low-status work than are men, and because women officeholders are comparatively rare, party leaders encountering a woman interested in political office could subconsciously assume that men are more likely to succeed in politics.

A number of evaluations were utilized to shed light on the prevalence of the distribution and outgroup effects in party chair attitudes. In the occupation ranking, the personality trait scale, women's electoral chances in different situations, the success of women over time, and in the gender of future candidates, party chairs did not strongly respond to the prevalence of the person's traits in politics. That is to say, their evaluations were not dependent on the distribution of an occupation in politics, the distribution of personality traits in politics, or the distribution of women in politics.

Conversely, party chairs displayed a consistent and significant preference for ingroup members over outgroup members using these same measures. Comparing the responses of male and female party chairs, males were found to be more positive toward occupations and traits associated with men and with candidates who were identified as being men. Concomitantly, female party chairs viewed female occupations, female traits, and female candidates more favorably.

Thus, the two major patterns that emerge from these multiple tests are both consistent with the outgroup effect. In other words, these patterns are consistent with the notion that party chairs make assumptions of positive similarity with ingroup members and not with the outgroup, exaggerate traits of the outgroup, and fail to individuate (or homogenize) the outgroup.

Given the aggregate findings that women reported experiencing bias and that aggregate patterns consistent with the outgroup effect were apparent, an individual-level measure was created to facilitate assessment of the determinants of these forms of bias. Individual-level data show the outgroup effect to be prevalent (with a majority appearing to be seriously influenced by it), while the distribution effect appears to be quite rare (about 3% seriously influenced by it).

A number of factors psychologists have identified as contributing to perceptual bias were adapted as independent variables in regression models assessing the determinants of the outgroup and distribution effects. The outgroup score regression model offers support for the role of outcome dependency, rigidity, power over outcomes, and exposure. The results indicate that having an uncertain electoral outcome, being less certain about one's assessments of candidates, not having power to enforce all of one's decisions in recruiting, and being exposed to a greater diversity of people and ideas (using indicators such as age and occupation) all decreased the propensity to utilize outgroup thinking in making assessments of potential candidates.

Perhaps the most significant implication of these findings centers on electoral competition. In short, believing the outcome is predetermined apparently creates an atmosphere conducive to bias regardless of whether victory or defeat is imminent. Close competition, on the other hand, which fosters great uncertainty about the impending outcome, represents a significant mitigating force, reducing outgroup scores. The significance of competition is that it would be hard or impossible for those external to the process and the people involved to change the recruiting power of a party chair or change that chair's confidence or life experiences. Electoral competition, on the other hand, is subject, if imperfectly, to the effects of state lawmakers. Campaign contribution laws and term limits are two of the most obvious recent statutory innovations that could affect competitiveness.

Rigidity and exposure were also significant determinants of the distribution effect. The other variable that reaches statistical significance is district ideology.

Party chairs in the most conservative districts have a higher distribution score than those in the most liberal districts. Thus, higher confidence in one's assessments, less diversity in life experiences, and conservative districts encourage the distribution effect. The distribution effect, in turn, encourages the positive evaluation of people based on their surface similarity to those who have previously succeeded, typically resulting in the devaluing of potential women candidates.

Ultimately, the significance of these findings rests on the effects of bias on women's candidacies. Reporting that women believe there is significant bias, finding party chair attitudes consistent with the outgroup effect, and isolating the determinants of bias are interesting only to the extent that this bias affects the process. Examining the determinants of women's legislative candidacies shows that women's political activity, inegalitarian mass attitudes, political culture (in the form of a history of women officeholders), and elite bias were all key factors. The finding that bias is a significant determinant of the number of women prospective candidates being considered by the party chair, as well as the likelihood that a woman would win a legislative seat nomination, is an important departure from previous research. In this analysis, both the outgroup effect and the distribution effect were associated with a reduction in the number of women prospective candidates and women nominees. The outgroup effect has by far the more substantial effect, with estimates showing its existence reducing women's candidacies by one-third in comparison to what would be expected with no bias. The exception to this pattern occurs in longshot districts, where bias slightly increases the likelihood of a male party chair recruiting a (essentially sacrificial) female candidate.

Finally, returning to the potential women candidates survey, results suggest that women who are best able to overcome bias are in some ways a different group, not representative of the universe of potential women candidates. Self-starters, those most likely to run in the face of party apathy or hostility, are more ideologically extreme. These self-starters are also less connected to women in that they describe themselves as being less focused on the importance of the women's vote, while having more typically male personality traits. In other words, the ultimate result of bias is more than limiting the number of women who run for legislative seats, it also entails limiting the type of women who run for legislative seats.

From potential women candidates' initial reports of bias and discriminatory treatment to their estimates of their career plans, from party chair perceptions of candidates and candidate traits to their recruiting plans, the evidence gleaned from these two groups of central actors in the recruitment process is consistently resonant with the notion that their interaction is affected by bias, a bias with real consequences for the candidacy rate and opportunity structure of women.

Generalizability of Study

With what breadth can these conclusions be applied, given the nature of the sample used? The results of this study are based on responses from county party chairs and locally-elected women. County party chairs are intended to serve as a sample of those involved in party recruitment. Clearly, county party chairs are not the sole actors in the recruitment process, nor are they always the dominant force in recruitment. However, they serve as a strong sample of party elites because they do tend to play a significant role in the recruitment of state legislative candidates (Frendreis et al. 1994; Frendreis, Gibson, and Vertz 1990), and because party elites, regardless of their specific position, tend to be a very homogeneous group (Patterson and Boynton 1970; Baer and Bositis 1988; Montjoy, Shaffer, and Weber 1980). Together, these findings suggest that party chairs are likely to be involved in the recruiting process and to be very much like the other elite participants in terms of background, attitudes, and behavior.[15]

Locally-elected women serve as a sample of potential legislative candidates. Some previous research has abandoned the effort to identify potential legislative candidates because of the inherent difficulties in identifying people based on their future activity. Locally-elected women, then, are a special group that has the interest and capability to contest for office on the legislative level in the future, but who are also identifiable. Of course, women holding local office are not the only source of legislative candidates, but they represent perhaps the most significant source (Carroll 1994; Hogan 1995) and are therefore a strong sample of potential legislative candidates.

This research was based on a survey of these two groups in four states: Ohio, New Jersey, Tennessee, and California. Are the findings indicative of patterns only in those four states, or are they applicable to the rest of the country? Two patterns suggest that the findings can be applied nationally. First, these are four diverse states, from different regions of the country, with quite different histories regarding the election of women and quite different state legislative structures. Second, the results for both the existence of bias and its effects show that the individual states are not significant determinants of bias. In other words, four diverse states, despite their obvious differences, produce quite consistent results with regard to the key measures examined here. If bias is found in such varied locations, it suggests that these patterns exist without regard to state boundaries.

Internal Validity

One of the fundamental requirements in the study of bias is disguising one's purpose. If a question deals with socially undesirable behavior, many will avoid the undesirable response regardless of the truth. Many measures in this study relied on questions with a hidden purpose. For example, that gender was the underlying concern in the evaluations of occupation and personality traits was obviously not clear to the respondents. In these cases, the nature of the questions augers well for the strength of the results as respondent corrections for social desirability do not seem plausible. Such measures were integral in the creation of the aggregate and individual-level assessments of the two forms of bias.

Many measures, of course, had obvious gender components. Some central conclusions, in fact, necessitated such measures. For example, the party chairs were asked the amount of women's party activity and the number of women future legislative candidates being considered. While both these questions solicit results that could reflect the effects of social desirability, this danger is reduced by utilizing independent assessments. The survey of potential women candidates provides a yardstick against which to measure chairs' estimates of such variables as women's party activity. Since these potential women candidates were not running their party, their party's situation would not reflect their attitudes, and they therefore would not need to protect themselves with socially desirable answers. Where applicable, estimates were compared, and in the case of women's party activity, were adjusted to reflect the input of potential women legislative candidates. Elsewhere, analysis of the number of women future legislative candidates, provided by party chairs, was repeated with women legislative nominees used as the dependent variable. By utilizing results provided independently, (in this case, election records or responses from women candidates), the results cannot be dismissed simply as socially desirable manipulation.

SCHOLARLY IMPLICATIONS

That the attitudes and behaviors of party chairs have consequences for potential women candidates obviously supports the simple notion that recruiting--notably who does the recruiting and what they think--is a significant component of the candidacy equation. Researchers, frequently utilizing case study or constricted settings in which to view the process of recruitment, have reported impressionistic evidence in support of the notion that recruitment matters (Fowler and McClure 1989; Canon, Schousen, and Sellers 1994; Abel and Oppenheimer 1994; Herrnson and Tennant 1994; Hertzke 1994; Kazee and Roberts 1994; Prewitt 1970; Hunt and Pendley 1972). Skeptics, frequently employing more broadly-based but less direct electoral result evidence, have raised doubts concerning the significance of recruiters in modern politics (Darcy, Welch, and Clark 1994). Utilizing survey methodology, as was done here, allows one to combine greater breadth of subjects (than the case study method can) with more attention to direct measures of the subjects' behaviors and attitudes (than most studies using electoral results can). Consequently, the case for the importance of recruitment is strengthened as the thrust of the results here complements the conclusions of those using the very different techniques of case study analysis.

Beyond the direct ramifications on involved women, to argue that party chairs express a preference for candidates who share surface similarities and harbor outgroup-based skepticism against those who are outwardly different has implications for all types of potential candidates. That is, the results suggest that the outgroup effect, which hurt women candidates in the eyes of male chairs, may have similar effects for those who are in different racial, ethnic, or even economic groups from the party leadership. It has been noted that the typical candidates who are encouraged, and who emerge on the state legislative level and above, in addition to being predominantly male, also reflect a lack of racial and economic diversity (Matthews 1984). This research, then, offers an additional potential explanatory factor for that pattern in the form of the outgroup effect among party leaders.

By virtue of arguing that recruitment matters, it is also hard to deny that political parties matter in the process of electing legislators. Even in a candidate-centered era, the modern party and its recruitment practices are relevant forces shaping our electoral choices. Moreover, as will be noted, the spread of term limits may serve chiefly to extend the power of parties.

While surveying county party chairs undeniably gives them the opportunity to claim importance, it is also true that virtually every state legislative seat in the country is held by members of the two major political parties. Thus, it is not surprising that parties provide the prime infrastructure for recruitment (Frendreis et al. 1994; Frendreis, Gibson, and Vertz 1990). If party chairs have significant influence on the candidacy process, they are therefore significantly affecting who the electorate can choose to vote for, and ultimately affecting who serves in office. As such, the importance of party chairs serves to remind us of the essential role of the un-elected in shaping our electoral process. These party chairs typically rise to their position by virtue of support from other party regulars. They do not assume their positions based on a public plebiscite, yet their decisions affect our electoral options and indirectly help shape our government. This strongly suggests that greater attention be paid by scholars to the role of party leaders (see, for example, Clarke and Kornberg 1979; Binning, Blumberg, and Green 1995). If party chairs are affecting the process, especially outside of the light of public attention, we should know more about how and from where these leaders emerge.

The lack of attention to party leadership and its genesis is especially surprising given the weight with which politicians have treated party leadership struggles. One of President John F. Kennedy's political aides, a veteran of Kennedy's races for the House, Senate, vice presidency, and presidency, said the Kennedy team's 1956 effort to reshape the leadership of the Massachusetts Democratic Party was "the most vicious fight I have ever experienced in all the years I have worked in politics" (quoted in Reeves 1991, 131). More recently, Binning, Blumberg, and Green (1995) documented the harsh struggle for power within the Mahoning County (OH) Democratic Party. Coupled with the results of this research, these examples of the significance that politicians place on control over party organizations suggest the value of more thorough study of party processes.

In addition to recruitment and political parties, these results also have relevance to the study of legislative politics. Scholars have noted differences in policy, priority, and style of conduct between male and female legislators (Rosenthal 1996; Berkman and O'Connor 1993; Kathlene 1995). The thrust of such research is that the number of women in a legislative body can be a significant determinant of what the legislature does and how it does it. To argue, then, that we have fewer women legislative candidates than we would have without biased elites, and that the women who persevere are somewhat less connected to women, is to argue that biased elites contribute to a process that makes our legislative bodies less consensual and less capable of focusing on the problems of a diverse population (Rosenthal 1996; Kathlene 1994). Further, this argument suggests that to change the makeup, behavior, and priorities of a state legislature, one important step is to change the people or the attitudes of the people involved in party recruitment.

Finally, this research also has implications for psychology and the political applications of psychological research. Use of psychological scholarship provided a foundation for the assumption that elites could be biased, and provided a map with which to find the origins of that bias, either in the outgroup or distribution effect. Clearly, utilization of psychological work added weight and perspective to a study that would have been much more limited if political science alone contributed to this research. Moreover, evidence and patterns quite consistent with the outgroup effect were, of course, found. Thus, the application of psychological work was not only useful as a means to think about the subject, but it was also successful as a means to produce evidence about the treatment of potential women candidates.

There are, undeniably, limitations in the use of psychological work. Specifically, the translation from psychological concept to political science operationalization is not always direct. While this study attempted to create political measures indicative of psychological patterns, clearly there is room for improvement, especially in studies that might focus specifically on the determinants of biased attitudes and thus be able to create more and better measures.

While psychology clearly contributed to this research, this research also makes some contribution to the study of psychology and political psychology. Utilizing theories born and tested in laboratories to study, understand, and explain the real-world behavior of political elites is part of the process of expanding our knowledge of these psychological processes. Psychological conclusions on the outgroup and distribution effects can be refined in the process of applying them to political actors, as evidence such as this amplifies or confounds laboratory findings.

For example, while the outgroup effect appears to have a stronger influence than the distribution effect on the behavior and attitudes of party chairs, studies of voter reaction to women candidates have been more likely to find attitudes consistent with the distribution effect (see, for example, Leeper 1991; Sapiro 1981b). This suggests that the power struggle inherent in party politics and candidate selection may foster competition and intense ingroup/outgroup distinctions that are less likely to surface in voters' decisions. Voters' preferences appear to be influenced by the distribution effect, perhaps not because of defensiveness or competition but because the voter's most obvious source of comparison for new candidates is not themselves but previous successful candidates. Beyond the prevalence of the distribution and outgroup effects, this research also explored the determinants of these effects. Here, the consistent connection between cognitive rigidity, outcome dependency, and the presence of the outgroup and distribution effects, tested in both bivariate and multivariate analyses, offers strong support to previous work that has found these traits to be important in the laboratory setting. Finally, by finding the outgroup and distribution effects to be significant determinants of the treatment of women candidates, this research underscores the value, for both psychologists and political scientists, of continued efforts to catalog and explain bias against groups of people.

IMPLICATIONS FOR WOMEN'S CANDIDACIES

The most daunting implication of the prevalence of bias in the form of the outgroup effect is that male party chairs will continue to express reluctance to support women regardless of the amount of success women candidates achieve. Unlike the distribution effect, which suggests negative evaluations of women would recede as women's success expanded, the outgroup effect offers no reason to expect that male party chairs will evolve into supporters of candidates who are unlike themselves. The outgroup effect persists because it is predicated on perceived distance. Distance does not recede with success of the outgroup, nor is success of the outgroup necessarily evidence of their merit. Instead, success for outgroup members can be treated as an isolated anomaly or explained away through situational events (Schlenker and Miller 1977).

While the central implication of the outgroup effect is rather pessimistic, there are some trends that foretell the possibility of major change. These trends involve competitiveness, term limits, and generational change.

Competitiveness

Competitiveness was found to reduce biased responses. Uncertainty of electoral outcome, in other words, increased the chairs' accuracy motivation and reduced their inclination to rely on perceptual bias. To the extent that more districts become competitive, there should be less bias against women in the future. If, however, competitiveness does not become more widespread or declines, women will not see such a positive effect. While the future of legislative races is not known, some important trends offer indications of the likely direction of elections. Among these trends are the increasing importance of legislative campaign committees and the likelihood of states adopting some form of campaign contribution limits.

Legislative campaign committees tend to emphasize the most competitive districts, offering vast sums of money to the races where the outcome is most in doubt (Gierzynski 1992) while ignoring the vast majority of districts. The overall effect of these efforts, then, is to divert money that might have once gone to a more typical district to the most competitive districts. In the process, typical districts are made somewhat less competitive as the candidates are left on their own (one usually with the overwhelming advantage of incumbency) to fight it out without any of the potentially leveling-out forces of the larger parties' resources.

At the same time, candidate contribution limits also serve to endanger competitiveness. By limiting the maximum contribution, states are reducing the incentive to contribute to underdog candidates, since a single limited contribution is unlikely to alter that candidate's electoral future (Box-Steffensmeier and Dow 1992). Marginalizing the effect of a single contribution thus encourages contributors to seek likely winners, in the process making likely winners stronger, likely losers weaker, and districts less competitive.

Term Limits

While both these factors suggest a reduction in competitiveness and its accompanying increase in bias, perhaps the largest looming effect will be that of term limits. Will term limits create great competitiveness by removing incumbents from the equation at regular intervals, or will the effects of party strength maintain imbalanced partisan competition in most districts? (see Aistrup 1993). Another possibility is that term limits could discourage competition by removing any incentive to challenge an incumbent, since an open seat will be available within a set number of years. Thus, term limits could create irregular patterns where competition exists only when potential terms are exhausted.

Scholars continue an active debate over the likely effects of term limits (see Reed and Schansberg 1995; Greene 1995; Jacobson 1995; Oppenheimer 1995; Clucas 1995). There is reason to expect term limits will increase competitiveness and there is reason to suspect term limits will not. Some who have contemplated the effects of term limits specifically on women candidates have suggested that term limits may result in a modest increase in women legislators by eliminating the most entrenched legislators who are predominantly male (Reed and Schansberg 1995; Thompson and Moncrief 1993; Akins 1996). Alternatively, term limits may severely damage the cause of electing women by preventing the relatively sparse group of successful women officeholders from continuing in their desired capacity as legislators (Leeper 1996). Still others have concluded that because of these conflicting forces, term limits may have virtually no effect on the number of women legislators (Clucas 1995), or that whatever effects term limits have they remain simply inestimable at this time (Jacobson 1995; Upshaw 1995).

While speculation and disagreement are prevalent in discussions of the effects of term limits, one aspect of term limits that produces a consensus is that term limits should increase the relative importance of parties in legislative competition (Reed and Schansberg 1995; Jacobson 1995). Instead of increasingly candidate-centered campaigns and organizations, as the tenure of incumbents is limited, parties will be left to provide continuity in districts. Moreover, the party leaders will personally have the opportunity to serve and shape their districts for longer periods than the legislative candidates they help elect. Any bias party leaders harbor, thus, would have magnified effects as their role in the political process grows.

While the debate continues over the effects of term limits on such matters as the number of open seats and the amount of competitiveness, it remains the case that openings themselves do not put women in office. Women must emerge from the process as legislative candidates. Regardless of how term limits affect the number of opportunities, term limits will not result in an increase in the number of women legislators merely by increasing the number of opportunities party chairs discourage women from pursuing.

Generational Change

Since competitiveness is endangered by legislative campaign committees and contribution limits, and since the effects of term limits include a likely expansion of the importance of party chairs, foreseeable political factors do not seem to bode well for increasing the number of women legislators. For optimism, one can turn to the personal determinants of bias.

Specifically, one factor that should make it easier for women to win the approval of party leaders is generational change. The year of birth of party chairs in the sample ranges from 1912 to 1972. In other words, it ranges from chairs who were born before women had won national suffrage to chairs who were born in the midst of the surge in women's consciousness and political power that produced, among other things, *The Feminine Mystique*, the National Organization for Women, and the push for the Equal Rights Amendment.

As the results in Chapter 5 indicate, younger chairs are significantly less likely to display outgroup bias, while older chairs prove to utilize significantly more perceptual bias. As younger cohorts continually replace the older chairs, party leaders should collectively become less inclined toward outgroup bias and more receptive to women candidates.

THE PARTY SOLUTION?

Since it is outgroup bias that appears to hurt women candidates most, one other important way to reduce bias against women, then, would be to increase the number of their ingroup members in party leadership--in other words, increase the number of women in positions of party power. While both major parties have professed interest in having more women run as candidates (Burrell 1994b), increasing the number of women party leaders has not been stressed. The number of women party chairs is slowly increasing (Baer 1993), and this bodes well for women candidates. However, women today still hold only a small minority of party chair positions.

While political parties or their leaders have been cast here as agents of exclusion, keeping multitudes of women from competing and contributing as candidates and officeholders, scholarship on parties does suggest that they could potentially be used as vehicles for inclusion. Many have viewed parties as a mechanism by which society's flaws and injustices can be challenged, where societal conflict can achieve political redress (see, for example, Ladd and Hadley 1975; Kirkpatrick 1978). As Broder (1971, xi) argued, "If we engage ourselves in politics, and particularly concern ourselves with the workings of those strangely neglected institutions, the political parties . . . we may find the instrument of national self-renewal in our hands." For this to happen, as Michels (1962 [1915], 172) once wrote, "It is an essential characteristic of democracy that every private carries a marshal's baton in his knapsack." In other words, there is great promise that in party action equitable outcomes are possible, but that effort will not come from an unencumbered elite but instead will rise with the furor and demands of average citizens who remove or reform the leadership.

Because of the collective opportunity to vote, new values--inclusive values--can be instilled by individuals who otherwise lack power. This applies not only to the choice of candidates in a primary but also to the choice of party leaders, a process which typically begins in primaries where party committee members are elected by the voters (those committee members later meet to select a chair). By actively participating in the selection of party leaders, under-represented groups can promote the development of new leaders, who force parties to recognize their constituency, which in turn promotes democracy (Baer and Bositis 1988).

Moreover, some scholars suggest that new leadership is in the parties' self-interest. Increasingly "torpid" leadership of local parties has weakened the parties' intermediary function (Burns 1980, 198), and consequently, parties have been unable to maintain their emotional bonds with voters, jeopardizing trust in the system (McWilliams 1980). The remedy awaits activists whose desire it is to communicate their discontent with the party system, by overthrowing local leaders and building new and more responsive parties (Lawson 1980).

This is the lure and promise of the process. Practically anyone can enter the process, and theoretically any large group will be heard because of the value of its number. The parties are not only open to new participants but they also need constant participation. This is the same promise, however, that this research concludes does not really exist for candidates. Because the party leaders do not encourage female candidacies, fewer occur. One could infer that party leaders are as, if not more, likely to discourage those who seek party leadership positions because of the potential threat to their own power. In fact, Baer and Bositis (1988) find that, in both parties, party chairs are opposed to rules that mandate equal roles for women in party leadership. Moreover, they argue that leaders see their dominance as right and proper and will fight any attempted insurrection (Baer and Bositis 1993). Or as Binning, Blumberg, and Green (1995, 31) see it, "Those in power clearly realize the value of controlling the party. The benefits are almost incalculable."

The idea takes on a rather cyclic nature--a group could take a dominant position in a party but they do not realize the strength of their position. They do not realize the strength of their position because challenges to party leadership are not encouraged and not common. The challenges are not common, of course, because groups do not realize the strength of their positions. Just as in the self-fulfilling nature of a legislative incumbent's success, where the perception of strength fends off strong challengers and the absence of strong challengers augers the perception of strength, this chain must be broken by those who realize both the severity and the promise of the situation.

Thus, two ideas must be communicated to women and those interested in women's participation and representation. First, the conclusions of research such as this must be presented. To wit, there is a significant problem in which the modus operandi of party leadership is inconsistent with the goal of increased women's representation (much less proportionate representation). Second is the notion that a takeover of party leadership can be accomplished. An excellent example (which will be discussed in detail) exists in the fight for control of the Mahoning County (OH) Democratic Party, where amateur party outsiders successfully captured the party infrastructure (Binning, Blumberg, and Green 1995).

Scholars who have studied the activation of women in a number of political pursuits emphasize the importance of communicating the severity of the problem. Especially useful is the framing of a problem in its most directly applicable terms. Morgen (1988), studying a women's health care coalition, finds that the impetus to organize and then participate collectively grew tremendously when the women involved began to feel that those in power had been explicitly dismissive in hearing the women's grievances. Similarly, in a study of an organization lobbying for public school building, Luttrell (1988) found a lingering problem without a response until a group of women were made aware of the scope of the funding imbalance and the plans officials were creating to make it potentially worse. Armed with collectively shocking and concrete information, a group of concerned women was able to create and sustain a successful political organization.

Nationally, the Clarence Thomas/Anita Hill hearings are considered important by many for their impact on women voters, specifically women's feelings that they lacked representation (Wilcox 1994). Women were no more excluded from the Senate during the Clarence Thomas/Anita Hill hearings than they had been for two centuries before, but the feeling of exclusion and having been dismissed was made more palpable by the hearings. Injustice alone will not necessarily spur political reaction, but when women are sufficiently disturbed by events, where they can see that their needs are being ignored, the opportunity for activism is enlarged.

Once the importance of the effort is established, belief in the potential success of the effort must be cultivated. Belief in success often hinges on the feeling that one is part of a group that seeks change rather than being merely a disgruntled individual. The notion that your group is being tread upon, and that it *collectively* can respond, foments group consciousness. As Shingles (1981) argues, group consciousness encourages political participation because it corresponds with internal efficacy and political mistrust. People who recognize *their group* has been treated unequally by the political system can blame the system rather than themselves. Since it is their group who is being hurt, their response does not have to be made alone but can be part of the unified response of the affected group. Together, these processes create motivation to seek change and enhance efficacy to believe such change is possible. Ultimately, such "group-conscious" individuals are empowered to participate in the political process (Sacks 1988; Zilber 1996; Cook 1987). For example, Zilber finds that group-conscious women are more likely to engage in high-cost political activities, such as campaigning for a candidate.

After activation by the callings of threat and promise, Kayden and Mahe (1985) argue that party activity can be sustained by solidary benefits and the quest for personal power. Numerous studies of women's political organizations relate the importance of friendship and social interaction (Sacks 1988; Mattison and Storey 1992; Luttrell 1988). Women who join a political organization for political reasons may often come to benefit from their participation more because they are surrounded by like-minded women whose company they enjoy. This process could prove critical after initial gains are recorded and the impetus for activity is weakening. Flammang (1984) notes the importance of regular gatherings for women's political organizations, as it allows women to create the same kind of political network that men have excluded them from.

The nature of political activity also offers the rewards of power to those who sustain their activity. Luttrell (1988) notes the example of women in the school building struggle who found that the organizing experience opened them up to the possibilities of their abilities. In turn, they were unwilling to give up the feeling that their contributions were unique and important. Sacks (1988) documents a similar process in a study of union formation. Women who organize successfully tend to enjoy the leadership task and seek to sustain the effort to allow them a continued venue to lead.

Getting Started

As it is generally in politics, it is the people who participate and offer their ideas who will be heard by political parties and their leaders (Marvick 1980). Kirkpatrick (1978) adds that because parties do not control access to their organizations, "it becomes possible for persons with little concern about the organization to achieve influence over its policies" (9). Ultimately, political parties "acquire principles almost accidentally" (Pomper 1992, 87).

As such, party leadership and power are not typically based on expertise or rank but instead revolve around competition between groups within the party that can result in upward mobility or downward mobility regardless of ability (Eldersveld 1964). Ultimately, the interpretation of any election is based on the key subgroups, whose participation and future support creates and sustains a leader's power. Collectively, then, the makeup of party leadership, the ideas of the parties, and the practices of parties are subject to the influence of any and all participants.

One straightforward implication of the notion that "who leads the party, leads the party's ideas" is the idea that if the parties are not friendly to women, it is a product of who happens to be in charge, not an inherent anti-women structure that infects parties. Leaders who assert their ingroup preferences with their group's support can be replaced as accidentally as they arrived.

In addition to the inability to control access to its organization, the vulnerability of parties to new groups, leaders, and ideas has origins in the fact that there is always more work to be done than workers to do it (Kirkpatrick 1978). It is thus easier for newcomers to achieve influence in a political party than in other types of organizations. New people are needed, new people are wanted, and new people can be influential if they come forward.

Importantly, new participants (from new groups) can be drawn not just from the pool of party activists, but potentially from all concerned citizens, including those who otherwise have no relationship or commitment to a political party. In fact, Kirkpatrick finds a healthy supply of activists in the parties who are there to support their agenda rather than the party itself. Such activists are characterized by a lack of agreement with traditional party practices including the need to compromise to win, the value of building diverse coalitions, and the importance of providing rewards for long-time party faithfuls. Instead, such participants seek the pursuit of their agenda to the exclusion of these "party-building" ideas.

One limitation for the goal of women's representation is that many argue that to achieve the goal of equal representation, women must do this work themselves. As Kirkpatrick writes, "In party reform, as in life, good intentions are never enough, and wishing does not make it so" (1978, 31). Thus, "genuine reform must come from interested parties rather than disinterested observers seeking to rationalize politics or make it more ethical" (Baer and Bositis 1993, 243). In other words, no one is capable of creating and sustaining equal treatment for women, other than women. Thus, the path to true outgroup power must be walked by members of the outgroup, members who see collective exclusion and the possibilities for change (Baer and Bositis 1993).

From where can like-minded women be found for this effort to join a movement to change party leadership? The best source is likely existing organizations with consonant purposes (Mattison and Storey 1992). For the goal of women's representation, women's groups are a model and a great source of grass-roots activism. A 1988 Women's Agenda Conference, for example, drew representatives of 40 national organizations with 15,000 local chapters (Baer and Bositis 1993). Sympathetic women who are prone to political action are thus accessible in those 15,000 chapters. In addition, a number of women's groups exist for the express purpose of aiding women's political endeavors, training women for leadership positions and helping organize women for political goals.[16]

Challenges to the Party Solution

Why are the women who have run for office and encountered bias not already collectively organized? One imagines that for these women personal observation and experience have not translated into collective observation and experience. That is, the women in the sample did not write of mass attacks on many women but on snide comments or exclusion that isolated them individually. Recall one woman's comment, "Throughout my political experience, there have always been various degrees of overlooking the women's opinion to hear what a man has to say. So ordinary, no one really notices."

Without collectively taking notice, these affected women were less likely to feel that they could successfully create change, as feelings of individual exclusion tend to limit efficacy (Baer and Bositis 1993). These women may have concluded that the effort to overthrow party leaders would not be successful, and that they may not personally be able to accomplish anything by trying. Sacks (1988) and Lutrell (1988), studying women's involvement in other political organizations, find a similar process where women were reluctant to assert their leadership abilities because they did not think there would be a receptive audience for them.

In sum, the problem for the women candidates organizing party revolutions is that those who do not feel discriminated against have no reason to think there is a problem, while those who have experienced discrimination may not think there is anything they can do about it. In short, the two key messages, that an important exclusionary problem exists and that women can unite to create change, are notably missing.

In fact, of those women in the sample who recounted mounting any kind of response to discriminatory treatment, none said that they did so as part of a group of affected women. Instead, typical comments suggested that their pique was expressed individually. For example, a California Democrat recounts, "I was told I was not qualified (as an attorney) to run, then the next three candidates were attorneys. I spoke to our county chair about the situation, but he wasn't really interested." One Ohio Republican lamented, "What can you do? You complain too much, then you're a whiner, and then they will never let you get ahead. I tell them [the county party] they are overlooking good candidates like me, when they favor their clique."

It must be noted, however, that challenges for taking over parties exist beyond those specific to women. Kayden and Mahe (1985) catalogue the difficulties of this type of endeavor. First, the "general low regard in which parties are held" (Kayden and Mahe 1985, 105) makes many uncomfortable with party politics and discourages activists from focusing their effort on partisan politics. Beyond that, there are other problematic facets of modern political parties. Kayden and Mahe emphasize two: the episodic nature of their function and the rise in importance of professional political service organizations. In parties, a lot of the time there is not much to do, and for short periods of time there is a tremendous amount to do. This schism makes it more challenging to hold the interest and commitment of activists. The professional pols also limit interest in party participation because they tend to dominate, making strategic input solely their function while downgrading local party organizations to lower-level functions (Shea 1995). Finally, Kayden and Mahe fear that the "decline of community" will also have chilling effects on party participation. Because we have less knowledge of our neighbors and are less willing to seek others out than previous generations, our modern mass media lifestyle feeds an isolation that may impede political organizing.

While the challenges for women candidates are admittedly great, and the challenges for women who wish to organize and take control of party leadership are similarly daunting, it must be underlined that there is hope. Women have collectively organized to create change, to create political institutions that are more inclusive and responsive to their needs (Sacks 1988; Luttrell 1988; Morgen 1988). Thus, while the effort required may be intimidating, successful efforts can achieve great outcomes.

Fundamentally, for any mass effort on women's behalf to succeed, two ideas must be explained, established, and ingrained in the concerned and affected. One, something must be done because women are being excluded in both a quantitative and qualitative way from having their voices heard in the electoral process. Two, something can be done to make parties more responsive, and ultimately the government more responsive, because the parties are open to new participants, and with enough new participants the parties will be open to those participants' beliefs and leadership. These ideas were effectively utilized in the battle for control of the Mahoning County Democratic Party.

The Mahoning County Example

An excellent example of the potential of motivated amateurs to assert themselves in party politics was documented in Binning, Blumberg, and Green's (1995) study of the Mahoning County Democratic Party, located near Youngstown, Ohio. Mahoning County had a strong and traditional Democratic Party, led by a county chair, Don Hanni, who after 16 years in that position was described as the consummate "insider politico." A group of disaffected Democrats began plotting to remove Hanni for, among other reasons, his preference for "old boy" politics, where endorsements and appointments went to loyalists instead of the most qualified individuals. Moreover, Hanni, a self-described "Archie Bunker," had publicly expressed his preference for candidates of his gender, race, and sexual orientation (Binning, Blumberg, and Green 1995, 9).

The chair of the county party is determined by a vote of the 409 precinct committee members in Mahoning County. The "Mahoning Democrats for Change" believed that the easiest way to oust the 16-year chair was to replace his loyalists on the precinct committee. Precinct committee positions were next to be contested on the May 1994 primary ballot. Traditionally, there had been no competition in these races, with the party leadership recruiting the only candidate in each precinct, and thereby securing that candidate's loyalty in the future.

The "Mahoning Democrats for Change" had a three-phase plan in their efforts to take over the party. First, in January and February they recruited candidates. They needed to identify supportive candidates in as many of the 409 precincts as possible, and they did this mostly by seeking sympathetic individuals who were not involved in party politics, but whose issue concerns could be addressed by the party and who were drawn to the purposive benefits of political activity. To underscore the outsider nature of most of the "change" candidates, 76% responded that they had not been "very active" in politics before the precinct race (Binning, Blumberg, and Green 1995, table 1).

After they built their slate of candidates, the next phase involved gathering resources for the fight ahead and building a campaign strategy. By April, all attention turned to communicating their campaign message to potential Democratic voters. The "change" team was able to raise as much money as a typical countywide candidate would, and they used it to paint the incumbent chair and his supporters as old pols who were out of touch with the community. The change ticket was able to use television and radio, as well as direct mail, to develop a two-pronged approach. First, they used negative messages designed to make people aware of the liabilities of Hanni, including his outlandish behavior and divisive personality. Second, the "change" ticket created positive/informational messages that were designed to make people aware of the change ticket and how to support them in the voting booth.

On Election Day, the change ticket won about two-thirds of the precinct races. With the previous leadership having had ties to the party insiders who had ruled the party for generations, the Mahoning Democrats for Change "traversed a century of history in a single night" (Binning, Blumberg, and Green 1995, 1). As previous research suggests, with the combination of a strong grievance and an outlet for political energies, people can unite to create party change. As Binning, Blumberg, and Green note, "extensive and sophisticated campaigns can be organized without a traditional party organization. Indeed, given enough provocation, something very much like a traditional party organization can be assembled in a short period of time and used with great effect" (1995, 41).

At a basic level, Binning, Blumberg, and Green conclude that county parties are "instruments for amassing and wielding power" (1995, 1). In this case, the "change" activists gained control of a party they saw as a vehicle for long-term interests, allowing them to influence politics and life in their community. By successfully orchestrating a takeover of county party politics, the Mahoning Democrats for Change made their county politics more inclusive and more responsive to the needs of the community. They also provide the blueprint for those in other counties who wish to see party leadership adapt to their needs.

By making the effort, the Mahoning County Democrats for Change defeated this county chair, and more importantly defeated his ideas, which favored candidates in his own image. Of course, the effort to take over the party was not easy. It required great numbers of candidates, volunteers, and contributors. While the parties may hold the key to the door of inclusion, it is a key that will certainly require the strength of a great many to turn.

As Flammang (1984, 111) asserts, women can unite to "challenge the ascendancy of the already powerful." They can, as the Mahoning Democrats for Change did, use the party as a tool to overcome the party. By changing a party, women gain a structural advantage that will facilitate women's inclusion as participants, party leaders, and candidates for public office. Rather than fighting for an individual woman candidate whose tenure may be short, the process of changing a party could produce a long-term ability to shape politics and influence our culture. As Binning, Blumberg, and Green (1995) conclude, there is a lot of power in the county party, and that is why it was sought after in Mahoning County, and that is why women should seek it in the larger effort to strengthen their electoral representation.

FINAL THOUGHTS

While this chapter offers some suggestions and reasons to believe improvement is possible, in essence this research finds potential women candidates report discrimination and party chairs offer attitudes consistent with bias. Most prominently in the form of the outgroup effect, this bias is associated with a one-third reduction in the number of women candidates. Bias was found to be most prevalent where the party chairs had power over the recruiting process, were relatively certain about the electoral outcome, were rigid in their thinking, and had less exposure to diversity. In the process, bias of party leaders produces fewer women legislative candidates, women candidates in weaker races, and women candidates who are less connected to women.

This research finds that, in the women's candidacy equation, elite bias matters. Unfortunately, the successful search for bias, like the search for Ahab's whale, is gratifying in only an ephemeral sense, as satisfaction can only accompany its elimination.

NOTES

1. California Republican.

2. New Jersey Republican.

3. Tennessee Republican.

4. California Democrat.

5. Tennessee Republican.

6. California Republican.

7. Ohio Democrat.

8. Ohio Republican.

9. Ohio Democrat.

10. Tennessee Democrat.

11. California Republican.

12. Ohio Democrat.

13. New Jersey Republican.

14. California Democrat.

15. Research on other actors in the recruitment process, such as Legislative Campaign Committees (LCCs), finds that while they may be active in select districts, in the vast majority of districts it is the county party that is the sole participant in recruitment (Shea 1995). Moreover, preliminary research on LCCs finds that they tend to draw candidates from a pool of activists that has been shaped by the local party (Niven 1997).

16. Specifically, the National Women's Political Caucus, the Women's Campaign Fund, and the YWCA Institute for Public Leadership all offer some assistance to women political activists. See Zepatos and Kaufman (1995) for a handbook on women's political activism.

Appendix A:
Cover Letter and Survey of
County Party Chairs

Respondents received the survey in the form of an eight page, 8.5" x 5.5" booklet, with the cover letter on a separate page.

Cover Letter

Ohio State University
Department of Political Science
2140 Derby Hall
Columbus, OH 43210

November 7, 1995

[respondent's name and address]

Dear County Chair:

I am engaged in a study to better understand the relationship between political party leaders and political candidates. As a current or recent county chair, I am writing to you to find out your views and to find out the role you undertake in the leader/candidate relationship. I would appreciate it very much if you would take a few minutes to fill out the enclosed questionnaire, and return it to me in the postage paid envelope. In order to pursue an accurate picture of this relationship, your response, regardless of your level of activity, is quite valuable.

Your name and address were kindly provided by your state party office. Moreover, you may be assured of complete confidentiality. Your name will never be placed on the questionnaire or used in any way.

The results of this research will contribute to a more complete understanding of how our system produces political candidates and officeholders, and how political party leaders, such as yourself, affect the process.

You may receive a summary of the results of this study by writing your name and address on the back of the return envelope, or by requesting a summary under separate cover. Please do not put this information on the questionnaire itself.

I would be most happy to answer any questions you might have. Please feel free to write, call, or fax.
Thank you for your assistance.

Sincerely,
David Niven

Survey

Please circle the number that corresponds to your answer, or write your answer on the lines provided. Scale endpoints (e.g., 1 = very strong, 5 = not strong) are meant as a guide, you should treat each number as an equal step from one side of the scale to the other.

Feel free to make any extra comments you have in the margins.

Your Party and the Electorate

Questions in this section deal with your party and its involvement in the recruitment of candidates for office. It is very important that you respond to these questions regardless of your party's level of activity in order to ensure that responses accurately represent the full range of county party activity in the process.

Please keep in mind that there are no right or wrong answers to these questions, we are simply seeking your expert opinion.

1. Overall, how strong would you say your county party organization is?
      1. VERY STRONG
      2.
      3.
      4.
      5. NOT STRONG

2. How important is it for your county party to receive the support of the following groups of voters?

	NOT IMPORTANT				VERY IMPORTANT
UNIONS	1	2	3	4	5
AFRICAN AMERICANS	1	2	3	4	5
SENIOR CITIZENS	1	2	3	4	5
WOMEN	1	2	3	4	5
YOUNG VOTERS (18-25)	1	2	3	4	5

3. Which state legislative district is most important to your county party organization. In other words, which district do you put the most effort into, or have the most influence in?

_____

4. Where would you place the voters of that state legislative district on the following ideological scale?

     1. VERY LIBERAL
     2.
     3.
     4. MODERATE
     5.
     6.
     7. VERY CONSERVATIVE

5. Where would you place the voters of that state legislative district on the following party support scale?

     1. STRONG DEMOCRATIC
     2.
     3.
     4.
     5.
     6.
     7. STRONG REPUBLICAN

6. Is the race in that state legislative district winnable for your party?

     1. NO
     2. YES

7. How competitive would you say the race between the two parties' candidates in that state legislative district will be?

     1. LOW
     2. MEDIUM
     3. HIGH

8. Do you expect your party to win that state legislative race?

     1. NO
     2. YES

9. For the following recruitment activities, please indicate whether or not your party performed the activity in the last 5 years, and if yes, how frequently.

Recruited state legislative candidates

       1. NO
       2. YES   How Often?   A. ONCE
                                   B. TWICE
                                   C. SEVERAL TIMES
                                   D. MANY TIMES

Discouraged a potential candidate in the county because you did not think they were qualified

       1. NO
       2. YES   How Often?   A. ONCE
                                   B. TWICE
                                   C. SEVERAL TIMES
                                   D. MANY TIMES

Discouraged a potential candidate because they did not fit the profile of a good candidate

       1. NO
       2. YES   How Often?   A. ONCE
                                   B. TWICE
                                   C. SEVERAL TIMES
                                   D. MANY TIMES

10. How much effort would you say you put into recruiting state legislative candidates?

       1. LOW
       2. MEDIUM
       3. HIGH

11. Please describe the typical recruiting process for state legislative candidates in your county. What is your role?

_____

_____

_____

_____

12. How well can you assess prospective state legislative candidates' potential strengths in the time you have to make a judgment?

        1. ASSESSMENTS NOT VERY ACCURATE
        2.
        3. ASSESSMENTS VERY ACCURATE

13. If your party was in need of a candidate for a special election or appointment for a state legislative seat, please think of the first five potential candidates that come to mind.

How many are men?
        1
        2
        3
        4
        5

Is the best candidate of the five a man?

        1. NO
        2. YES

14. Comparing an average female legislative candidate in your state ten years ago, with an average female candidate today, how would you characterize their relative chances for victory?

        1. BETTER CHANCE TEN YEARS AGO
        2.
        3.
        4. SAME
        5.
        6.
        7. BETTER CHANCE TODAY

15. Of the people who play an active role in your county party, attending meetings or contributing to your party in other significant ways, approximately what percentage are women?

        _____%

16. Approximately what percentage of officeholders in your county are women?

        _____%

Background and Political Life

This section of questions asks for some basic information on your background and political experiences.

17. What is your political party?

> 1. REPUBLICAN
> 2. DEMOCRATIC

18. Have you ever held any elected public office?

> 1. NO
> 2. YES
>
> IF YES,
> WHICH OFFICES_____

19. During what years have you been county party chair?

_____

20. Where would you place yourself on the following ideological scale?

> 1. VERY LIBERAL
> 2.
> 3.
> 4. MODERATE
> 5.
> 6.
> 7. VERY CONSERVATIVE

21. What is your year of birth?

____

22. In what state were you born?

____

23. What is your gender?

> 1. MALE
> 2. FEMALE

24. What is your race?

_____

25. What is the highest level of education you have completed?

       1. GRADE SCHOOL
       2. HIGH SCHOOL
       3. SOME COLLEGE
       4. COLLEGE
       5. ADVANCED DEGREE

26. Were there any family members who were influential in   creating your political interests? If yes, which members of your family?

_____

_____

_____

27. Have you had a primary occupation outside politics?

       1. NO
       2. YES

         IF YES,
         WHAT WAS IT?_____

Views on Candidates

Questions in this section ask you to evaluate traits people who run for office might display. Again, there are no right or wrong answers to these questions.

28. Here we would like to know how you would respond to the idea of candidates with different occupational backgrounds. If could know only their profession, please tell us how enthusiastic you would be about the prospect of a person with these occupational backgrounds coming forward as a state legislative candidate by ranking the following list in order from 1 to 7 (1 = least favorable, 7 = most favorable).

LAWYER   __

GRADE SCHOOL TEACHER   __

TELEVISION REPORTER   __

SALES   __

FORMER ATHLETE   __

POLICE OFFICER   __

SOMEONE WITH YOUR
    PRIMARY OCCUPATION   __

29. Now we turn to evaluating candidates with certain personality traits. Please tell us how important the following traits are in your personal assessment of a potential candidate's ability to win a seat in the state legislature, first by noting if the trait is positive or negative, and second by rating how important you think that trait is on a scale from 1 to 7 (1 = not important at all, 7 = very important).

		1 = not important 7 = important
individualistic	positive_____ negative_____	1 2 3 4 5 6 7
compassionate	positive_____ negative_____	1 2 3 4 5 6 7
tactful	positive_____ negative_____	1 2 3 4 5 6 7
cautious	positive_____ negative_____	1 2 3 4 5 6 7
competitive	positive_____ negative_____	1 2 3 4 5 6 7
serious	positive_____ negative_____	1 2 3 4 5 6 7
modest	positive_____ negative_____	1 2 3 4 5 6 7
arrogant	positive_____ negative_____	1 2 3 4 5 6 7
adaptable	positive_____ negative_____	1 2 3 4 5 6 7
aggressive	positive_____ negative_____	1 2 3 4 5 6 7
unpredictable	positive_____ negative_____	1 2 3 4 5 6 7
yielding	positive_____ negative_____	1 2 3 4 5 6 7
conventional	positive_____ negative_____	1 2 3 4 5 6 7
loyal	positive_____ negative_____	1 2 3 4 5 6 7
outspoken	positive_____ negative_____	1 2 3 4 5 6 7

30. Finally, we would like to know your assessment of the chances for election of candidates with particular features if they were running in the general election in your county. Using your expertise, please offer an educated guess on the chances for winning election on a scale of 0-100 (with 0 representing no chance of election, and 100 representing certain election).

A woman challenger from your party, running on mainstream issues of your area:

chance of victory in town/city council race   _____

chance of victory in state house race   _____

chance of victory in congressional race   _____

A woman challenger from your party, running on women's issues:

chance of victory in town/city council race   _____

chance of victory in state house race   _____

chance of victory in congressional race   _____

A woman incumbent from your party, running on mainstream issues of your area:

chance of victory in town/city council race   _____

chance of victory in state house race   _____

chance of victory in congressional race   _____

A woman incumbent from your party, running on women's issues:

chance of victory in town/city council race   _____

chance of victory in state house race   _____

chance of victory in congressional race   _____

Thank you very much.
Please fold survey and return in the postage paid envelope.
If envelope is lost, survey may be returned to:
David Niven, Ohio State University
Department of Political Science
2140 Derby Hall, Columbus OH 43210

Appendix B:
Cover Letter and Survey of Potential Women Candidates

Respondents received the survey in the form of an eight page, 8.5" x 5.5" booklet, with the cover letter on a separate page.

Cover Letter:

Ohio State University
Department of Political Science
2140 Derby Hall
Columbus, OH 43210

November 7, 1995

[respondent's name and address]

Dear Madam:

I am engaged in a study to better understand the relationship between political party leaders and political candidates. I would appreciate it very much if you would take a few minutes to fill out the enclosed questionnaire, and return it to me in the postage paid envelope. In order to pursue an accurate picture of this relationship, your response, regardless of your type of office or amount of contact with party leaders, is quite valuable.

Your name and address were kindly provided by the National League of Cities. Moreover, and you may be assured of complete confidentiality. Your name will never be placed on the questionnaire or used in any way.

The results of this research will contribute to a more complete understanding of how our system produces political candidates and officeholders. You may receive a summary of the results of this study by writing your name and address on the back of the return envelope, or by requesting a summary under separate cover. Please do not put this information on the questionnaire itself.

I would be most happy to answer any questions you might have. Please feel free to write, call, or fax. Thank you for your assistance.

Sincerely,

David Niven

Survey

Please circle the number that corresponds to your answer, or write your answer on the lines provided.

Scale endpoints (e.g., 1 = very involved, 5 = not involved) are meant as a guide, you should treat each number as an equal step from one side of the scale to the other.

Feel free to make any extra comments you have in the margins

Political Life
This section of questions asks for some basic information on your political experiences.

1. What is your political party?

> 1. REPUBLICAN
> 2. DEMOCRATIC

2. What type of office do you hold?

_____

3. Approximately what size constituency do you represent?

_____

4. When did you first run for office?

_____

5. How involved was your political party in encouraging your first run for office?

     1. VERY INVOLVED
     2.
     3.
     4.
     5. NOT INVOLVED

6. How involved has your political party been in shaping your political career decisions?

     1. VERY INVOLVED
     2.
     3.
     4.
     5. NOT INVOLVED

7. We would like to know something about your potential political future. Using a scale of 0 to 100 (0 meaning no chance, 100 meaning certainty), please indicate the likelihood of you deciding to run for the state house in your district under the following conditions.

"You are interested in running and you are being recruited by your party to run"
     ____%chance

"You are interested in running, but not being recruited by your party"
     ____%chance

"You are interested in running, but you are being discouraged from running by your party"

     ____%chance

8. Where would you place yourself on the following ideological scale?
     1. VERY LIBERAL
     2.
     3.
     4. MODERATE
     5.
     6.
     7. VERY CONSERVATIVE

9. Please rate the desirability of the following government responses to the status of women in the U.S.

	Not Desirable		Very Desirable
Equal Rights Amendment	1	2 3 4 5 6	7
More Strict Enforcement of Sexual Harassment	1	2 3 4 5 6	7
Affirmative Action programs to benefit women	1	2 3 4 5 6	7

Background
We now turn to a few questions on your life.

10. What is your year of birth?

——

11. In what state were you born?

——

12. What is your race?

——

13. What is the highest level of education you have completed?

1. GRADE SCHOOL
2. HIGH SCHOOL
3. SOME COLLEGE
4. COLLEGE
5. ADVANCED DEGREE

Electorate in Your Area
This section asks for your assessment of the voters' attitudes.

14. Where would you place the voters of your state legislative district on the following ideological scale?

      1. VERY LIBERAL
      2.
      3.
      4. MODERATE
      5.
      6.
      7. VERY CONSERVATIVE

15. Where would you place the voters of your state legislative district on the following party support scale?

      1. STRONG DEMOCRATIC
      2.
      3.
      4.
      5.
      6.
      7. STRONG REPUBLICAN

16. How important is it for your county party to receive the support of the following groups of voters?

	NOT IMPORTANT				VERY IMPORTANT
UNIONS	1	2	3	4	5
AFRICAN AMERICANS	1	2	3	4	5
SENIOR CITIZENS	1	2	3	4	5
WOMEN	1	2	3	4	5
YOUNG VOTERS (18-25)	1	2	3	4	5

17. As a politically active person, we would like to know your assessment of the chances for election of candidates with particular features if they were running in the general election in your home county. Using your expertise, please offer an educated guess on the chances for winning election on a scale of 0-100 (with 0 representing no chance of election, and 100 representing certain chance of election). There are no right or wrong answers.

A woman challenger from your party, running on the mainstream issues of your area:

chance of victory in town/city council race   _____
chance of victory in state house race   _____
chance of victory in congressional race   _____

A woman challenger from your party, running on the women's issues:

chance of victory in town/city council race   _____
chance of victory in state house race   _____
chance of victory in congressional race   _____

A woman incumbent from your party, running on the mainstream issues of your area:

chance of victory in town/city council race   _____
chance of victory in state house race   _____
chance of victory in congressional race   _____

A woman incumbent from your party, running on the women's issues:

chance of victory in town/city council race   _____
chance of victory in state house race   _____
chance of victory in congressional race   _____

18. Next, we would like to know what qualities you think the electorate in your district looks for in good state legislative candidates. Please tell us how important you believe the following traits are in the electorate's assessment of candidates for the state legislature, first by noting if the trait is positive or negative, and second by rating how important you think that trait on a scale from 1 to 7 (1 = very important, 7 = not important at all). Again, there are no right or wrong answers, we are simply seeking your opinion.

		1 = not important 7 = important
individualistic	positive_____ negative	1 2 3 4 5 6 7
compassionate	positive_____ negative	1 2 3 4 5 6 7
tactful	positive_____ negative	1 2 3 4 5 6 7
cautious	positive_____ negative	1 2 3 4 5 6 7
competitive	positive_____ negative	1 2 3 4 5 6 7
serious	positive_____ negative	1 2 3 4 5 6 7
modest	positive_____ negative	1 2 3 4 5 6 7
arrogant	positive_____ negative	1 2 3 4 5 6 7
adaptable	positive_____ negative	1 2 3 4 5 6 7
aggressive	positive_____ negative	1 2 3 4 5 6 7
unpredictable	positive_____ negative	1 2 3 4 5 6 7
yielding	positive_____ negative	1 2 3 4 5 6 7
conventional	positive_____ negative	1 2 3 4 5 6 7
loyal	positive_____ negative	1 2 3 4 5 6 7
outspoken	positive_____ negative	1 2 3 4 5 6 7

Party Organization

Questions in this section deal with your experiences and observations of your political party. It is very important that you respond to these questions regardless of your contact with your party in order to ensure that responses accurately represent the range of experiences candidates have had.

19. In your experience, have party leaders discouraged potential women candidates from running for office because of their gender?

> 1. NO
> 2. YES

If there are any specific instances that come to mind where gender has affected the treatment women received in party politics, please describe in the space provided.

_____

_____

_____

_____

_____

20. In general, are the women active in your political party less qualified, more qualified, or equally qualified to run for office in comparison to the active men?

> 1. WOMEN LESS QUALIFIED
> 2. WOMEN EQUALLY QUALIFIED
> 3. WOMEN MORE QUALIFIED

21. Of the people who play an active role in your county party, approximately what percentage are women?

_____ %

22. Approximately what percentage of officeholders in your county are women?

_____ %

29. Finally, we would like to know how well each of these politically relevant traits describes *you*. Please offer your own assessment on whether each trait describes you very well or not well at all by circling the appropriate number on a scale from 1 to 7 (1 = very characteristic of you, 7 = not characteristic of you).

	1=not characteristic 7=very characteristic
individualistic	1 2 3 4 5 6 7
compassionate	1 2 3 4 5 6 7
tactful	1 2 3 4 5 6 7
cautious	1 2 3 4 5 6 7
competitive	1 2 3 4 5 6 7
serious	1 2 3 4 5 6 7
modest	1 2 3 4 5 6 7
arrogant	1 2 3 4 5 6 7
adaptable	1 2 3 4 5 6 7
aggressive	1 2 3 4 5 6 7
unpredictable	1 2 3 4 5 6 7
yielding	1 2 3 4 5 6 7
conventional	1 2 3 4 5 6 7
loyal	1 2 3 4 5 6 7
outspoken	1 2 3 4 5 6 7

Thank you very much.
Please fold survey and return in the postage paid envelope.

If envelope is lost, survey may be returned to:
David Niven
Ohio State University
Department of Political Science
2140 Derby Hall
Columbus OH 43210

Appendix C:
Correlations of Independent Variables in Determinants of Bias Models

Key:

Outcome Dependency
Competitiveness of District   COMP
Winnable Race   OUT

Accountability
Tenure as Chair   YEARCH
Recruiting Effort   REC

Cognitive Rigidity
Confidence in Candidate Assessments   CANASS
Discourage Unqualified Candidates   DISC UNQ
Discourage Poor Profile Candidates   DISC PRO

Power over Outcome
Recruiting Power   POWER
Strength of Party Organization   PARORG
Expect to Win Next Legislative Election   WIN

Time Pressure
Time to Evaluate Recruits   TIME

Exposure/Personal Background
Age   YEARB
Family   WFAM
Education   CEDUC
Occupation   OCCUP
Ideology   CIDEOL

Controls
District Ideology   DIDEOL
Party   PARTY
California   CAL
New Jersey   NJ
Ohio   OH
Party Chair Gender   CSEX

```
Correlations:  COMP        OUT       YEARCH        REC       CANASS      DISC UNQ

COMP         1.0000
OUT          -.3901**    1.0000
YEARCH        .0510      -.0346     1.0000
REC           .1743       .0050     -.1029      1.0000
CANASS        .0966      -.0112     -.0112      -.0647      1.0000
DISC UNQ     -.0238      -.0602     -.1368       .0121      -.1147      1.0000
DISC PRO      .1031      -.0549     -.0640       .2954**    -.0794       .3348**
POWER         .0933       .1085     -.1138       .2725**    -.0176       .1073
PARORG       -.0784       .2818**    .1649      -.1407       .1314      -.0591
WIN          -.4415**    -.2025**    .0247      -.2138*     -.0901       .1051
TIME          .0541       .0059     -.1252       .3159**    -.1343       .1500
ELECOFF      -.0740      -.0118     -.0292      -.0938       .1278       .0516
YEARB        -.1492       .1452      .3243**     .0187       .1263      -.0436
WFAM          .0536       .0270      .0332       .0539      -.0838       .0010
CEDUC         .0307      -.0395      .0763      -.0020      -.0758       .0378
OCCUP        -.0666       .0045     -.0969       .0085       .0397       .0327
CIDEOL       -.0267      -.1425      .0173       .0861       .0567      -.0374
DIDEOL       -.0644       .0606      .0386      -.0164      -.0140      -.0995
PARTY        -.1244       .1457     -.0018      -.0753      -.0548       .0967
CSEX         -.0409       .0235      .0305       .0639      -.0155      -.0494
CAL          -.0509       .0639      .1490      -.1280      -.0018      -.0168
NJ            .1153       .0790     -.0156       .0667      -.0891       .1806*
OH            .1541       .0466     -.2732**     .1836*      .0984      -.0814


Correlations:  DISC PRO    POWER     PARORG        WIN        TIME

DISC PRO     1.0000
POWER         .1035      1.0000
PARORG       -.0302      -.0994     1.0000
WIN          -.0586      -.0203     -.3294**    1.0000
TIME          .1483       .4555**   -.1443      -.1290      1.0000
YEARB        -.0979      -.0758      .0451      -.0012      -.0278
WFAM          .1616       .1514     -.0520       .0628       .0473
CEDUC         .1683       .0072      .0216       .0163       .0349
OCCUP        -.0776      -.1073     -.0524       .0153      -.1138
CIDEOL       -.0335       .0394     -.1835*      .1554       .0233
DIDEOL       -.0585      -.1083      .0719       .0610      -.1464
PARTY        -.0309      -.0399      .2561**    -.2300**    -.0307
CSEX         -.0265      -.0378     -.0235       .0239      -.0831
CAL           .0389       .0294      .1875*      .0297      -.0624
NJ            .0478       .1097     -.0910       .1052       .2105*
OH            .0429       .1765*    -.0784       .0192       .1038


Correlations:  YEARB       WFAM       CEDUC        OCCUP      CIDEOL

YEARB        1.0000
WFAM         -.0829      1.0000
CEDUC         .2385**     .2321**   1.0000
OCCUP         .2347**    -.0494      .4280**    1.0000
CIDEOL       -.0318      -.1176     -.1706       .1315      1.0000
DIDEOL       -.0785      -.0998     -.0904       .1139       .2675**
PARTY         .0003       .0467      .0844      -.1076      -.4862**
CSEX          .0531       .0363     -.1587      -.0066      -.1720*
CAL           .0134       .0565      .0079      -.0723      -.1508
NJ           -.0003      -.0494      .0042      -.0737      -.0474
OH            .1926*      .1073     -.0147       .0955      -.0222
```

```
Correlations:  DIDEOL     PARTY       CSEX

  DIDEOL       1.0000
  PARTY        -.1899*    1.0000
  CSEX         -.0721      .0992     1.0000
  CAL          -.1985*     .0415      .0456
  NJ           -.0590      .0794     -.1072
  OH            .0514     -.0358      .0983

Minimum pairwise N of cases:   255          2-tailed Signif:  *p < .01   **p < .001
```

Appendix D:
Correlations of Independent Variables in Determinants of Women's Candidacy Rate Models

Key:

Elite Bias

Outgroup Score   OUTGRP

Distribution Score   DISTRB

Bias/Longshot Race   LONSHT

Women

Women Party Activity   WOMPAR

Mass Behavior

Non-Egalitarian Attitudes   EGALATT

Political Culture   POLCUL

Party Dominance

Party   PARTY

Strength of Party Organization   PARORG

Electoral Competitiveness   COMP

State Variation

California   CAL

New Jersey   NJ

Ohio   OH

```
Correlations:  OUTGRP     DISTRB     LONSHT     WOMPAR     EGALATT    POLCUL

     OUTGRP    1.0000
     DISTRB    -.0396     1.0000
     LONSHT     .3763**   -.1684     1.0000
     WOMPAR    -.0989      .0573     -.1008     1.0000
     EGAATT     .1534      .0104      .2230**   -.1174     1.0000
     POLCUL     .2297**   -.0169      .2171**   -.1981*     .0439     1.0000
     PARTY     -.0806      .0938     -.0825      .1230     -.3181**   -.0988
     PARORG     .0909      .1479     -.0715      .1680      .0587     -.0641
     COMP      -.0175     -.0184      .0841     -.0787      .1486     -.0777
     CAL       -.0204      .0522     -.0968      .2138*     .0419      .1160*
     NJ         .0279      .0366     -.0555     -.1091     -.1056     -.1090
     OH        -.2377**    .0979     -.1828*    -.0747      .0722     -.0112

Correlations:  PARTY      PARORG     COMP

     PARTY     1.0000
     PARORG     .2561**   1.0000
     COMP      -.1244     -.0784     1.0000
     CAL        .0415      .1875*    -.0509
     NJ         .0794     -.0910      .1153
     OH        -.0358     -.0784      .1541

Minimum pairwise N of cases:   255          2-tailed Signif:   * - .01   ** - .001
```

Bibliography

Abel, D., and B. Oppenheimer. (1994) "Candidate Emergence in a Majority Hispanic District: The 29th District in Texas." In *Who Runs for Congress?*, T. Kazee (ed.). Washington, DC: Congressional Quarterly Press.

Achen, C. (1982) *Interpreting and Using Regression*. Sage University Paper Series on Quantitative Application in the Social Sciences, 07-029. Beverly Hills, CA: Sage Publications.

Agnew, C., V. Thompson, V. Smith, R. Gramzow, and D. Currey. (1993) "Proximal and Distal Predictors of Homophobia: Framing the Multivariate Roots of Outgroup Rejection." *Journal of Applied Social Psychology* 23: 2013-2042.

Aistrup, J. (1993) "State Legislative Party Competition: A County Level Measure." *Political Research Quarterly* 46: 433-446.

Akins, F. (1996) "Access to Legislative Institutions: A Multivariate Analysis of the Presence of Women in State Legislatures in 1995." Presented at the Annual Meeting of the Southern Political Science Association.

Alexander, D., and K. Andersen. (1993) "Gender as a Factor in the Attribution of Leadership Traits." *Political Research Quarterly* 46: 527-545.

Ambrosius, M., and S. Welch. (1984) "Women and Politics at the Grassroots: Women Candidates for State Office in Three States, 1950-1978." *Social Science Journal* 21: 29-42.

Andersen, K., and E. Cook. (1985) "Women, Work, and Political Attitudes." *American Journal of Political Science* 29: 606-622.

Andersen, K., and S. Thorson. (1984) "Congressional Turnover and the Election of Women." *Western Political Quarterly* 37: 143-156.

Arrighi-Merz, B. (1991) "Control in the Workplace: Its Determinants and Its Effects on Political Behavior and the Domestic Division of Labor." Ph.D. dissertation, University of Cincinnati.

Baer, D. (1993) "Political Parties: The Missing Variable in Women and Politics Research." *Political Research Quarterly* 46: 547-576.

Baer, D., and D. Bositis. (1988) *Elite Cadres and Party Coalitions: Representing the Public in Party Politics*. Westport, CT: Greenwood Press.

Baer, D., and D. Bositis. (1993) *Politics and Linkage In a Democratic Society*. Englewood Cliffs, NJ: Prentice-Hall.

Bem, S. (1974) "The Measurement of Psychological Androgyny." *Journal of Consulting and Clinical Psychology* 42: 155-162.

Bem, S., and D. Bem. (1970) "Case Study of a Nonconscious Ideology: Training the Woman to Know Her Place." In *Beliefs, Attitudes, and Human Affairs*, D. Bem (ed.). Belmont, CA: Brooks/Cole Publishing.

Bennett, L. (1986) "The Gender Gap: When an Opinion Gap Is Not a Voting Bloc." *Social Science Quarterly* 67: 613-625.

Bennett, S., and L. Bennett. (1992) "From Traditional to Modern Conceptions of Gender Equality in Politics." *Western Political Quarterly* 45: 93-111.

Benze, J., and E. Declercq. (1985) "The Importance of Gender in Congressional and Statewide Elections." *Social Science Quarterly* 66: 954-963.

Berkman, M., and R. O'Connor. (1993) "Do Women Legislators Matter? Female Legislators and State Abortion Policy." *American Politics Quarterly* 21: 102-124.

Bernstein, R. (1986) "Why Are There So Few Women in the House?" *Western Political Quarterly* 39: 155-164.

Biersack, R., and P. Herrnson. (1994) "Political Parties and the Year of the Woman." In *The Year of the Woman: Myths and Realities*, E. Cook, S. Thomas, and C. Wilcox (eds.). Boulder, CO: Westview Press.

Binning, W., M. Blumberg, and J. Green. (1995) "Change Comes to Steeltown: Local Political Parties as Instruments of Power." Presented at the Annual Meeting of the American Political Science Association.

Black, G. (1972) "A Theory of Political Ambition: Career Choices and the Role of Structural Incentives." *American Political Science Review* 66: 114-159.

Blair, D., and A. Henry. (1981) "The Family Factor in State Legislative Turnover." *Legislative Studies Quarterly* 6: 55-68.

Bledsoe, T., and M. Herring. (1990) "Victims of Circumstances: Women in Pursuit of Political Office." *American Political Science Review* 84: 215-223.

Bowman, L., and G. Boynton. (1971) "Recruitment Patterns Among Local Party Officials: A Model and Some Preliminary Findings in Selected Locales." In *A Comparitive Study of Party Organizations*, W. Wright (ed.). Columbus, OH: Merrill Publishing.

Box-Steffensmeier, J., and J. Dow. (1992) "Campaign Contributions in an Unregulated Setting: An Analysis of the 1984 and 1986 California Assembly Elections." *Western Political Quarterly* 44: 609-628.

Breaux, D., and A. Gierzynski. (1991) "It's Money that Matters: Campaign Expenditures and State Legislative Primaries." *Legislative Studies Quarterly* 16: 429-443.

Briscoe, J. (1989) "Perceptions that Discourage Women Attorneys from Seeking Public Office." *Sex Roles* 21: 557-567.

Broder, D. (1971) *The Party's Over*. New York: Harper and Row.

Brooks, R. (1995) "The Influence of Paid Employment on Women's Political Participation." Presented at the Annual Meeting of the Midwest Political Science Association.

Brown, J., R. Collins, and G. Schmidt. (1988) "Self-Esteem and Direct Versus Indirect Forms of Self-Enhancement." *Journal of Personality and Social Psychology* 55: 445-453.

Browning, R. (1968) "The Interaction of Personality and Political System in Decisions to Run for Office." *Journal of Social Issues* 24: 93-109.

Bullock, C., and P. Heys. (1972) "Recruitment of Women for Congress." *Western Political Quarterly* 25: 416-423.

Bullock, C., and L. Johnson. (1985) "Sex and the Second Primary." *Social Science Quarterly* 66: 933-944.

Bullock, C., and S. MacManus. (1991) "Municipal Electoral Structure and the Election of Councilwomen." *Journal of Politics* 53: 75-89.

Burns, J.M. (1980) "Party Renewal: The Need for Intellectual Leadership." In *Party*

Renewal in America, G. Pomper (ed.). New York: Praeger.

Burrell, B. (1988) "The Political Opportunity Structure of Women Candidates for the U.S. House of Representatives in 1984." *Women and Politics* 8: 51-68.

Burrell, B. (1990) "The Presence of Women Candidates and the Role of Gender in Campaigns for the State Legislature in an Urban Setting." *Women and Politics* 10: 85-102.

Burrell, B. (1992) "Women Candidates in Open-Seat Primaries for the U.S. House: 1968-1990." *Legislative Studies Quarterly* 17: 493-508.

Burrell, B. (1993) "John Bailey's Legacy: Political Parties and Women's Candidacies for Public Office." In *Women in Politics: Outsiders or Insiders?*, L. Duke (ed.). Englewood Cliffs, NJ: Prentice Hall.

Burrell, B. (1994a) *A Woman's Place Is in the House: Campaigning for Congress in the Feminist Era.* Ann Arbor: University of Michigan Press.

Burrell, B. (1994b) "Women's Political Leadership and the State of the Parties." In *The State of the Parties*, D. Shea and J. Green (eds.). Lanham, MD: Rowman and Littlefield.

Burt-Way, B., and R. Kelly. (1991) "Gender and Sustaining Political Ambition." *Western Political Quarterly* 44: 11-25.

Byrne, G., and J. Pueschel. (1974) "But Who Should I Vote for for County Coroner?" *Journal of Politics* 36: 778-784.

Cable, S. (1992) "Women's Social Movement Involvement: The Role of Structural Availability in Recruitment and Participation Processes." *The Sociological Quarterly* 33: 34-50.

Caldeira, G., and S. Patterson. (1982a) "Contextual Influences on Participation in U.S. State Legislative Elections." *Legislative Studies Quarterly* 7: 359-381.

Caldeira, G., and S. Patterson. (1982b) "Bringing Home the Votes." *Political Behavior* 4: 33-67.

Canon, D., M. Schousen, and P. Sellers. (1994) "A Formula for Uncertainty: Creating a Black Majority District in North Carolina." In *Who Runs for Congress?*, T. Kazee (ed.). Washington, DC: Congressional Quarterly Press.

Carpenter, S. (1993) "Organization of In-Group and Out-Group Information: The Influence of Gender-Role Information." *Social Cognition* 11: 70-91.

Carroll, S. (1985) "Political Elites and Sex Differences in Political Ambition: A Reconsideration." *Journal of Politics* 1231-1243.

Carroll, S. (1994) *Women as Candidates in American Politics.* Bloomington, IN: Indiana University Press.

Carroll, S., and W. Strimling. (1983) *Women's Routes to Elective Office: A Comparison with Men's.* New Brunswick, NJ: Eagleton Institute of Politics.

Carver, J. (1979) "Women in Florida." *Journal of Politics* 41: 941-955.

Clark, J., and C. Clark. (1984) "The Growth of Women's Candidacies for Nontraditional Political Offices in New Mexico." *Social Science Journal* 21: 57-66.

Clark, J., R. Darcy, S. Welch, and M. Ambrosius. (1984) "Women as Legislative Candidates in Six States." In *Political Women*, J. Flammang (ed.). Beverly Hills, CA: Sage Publications.

Clark, J., C. Hadley, and R. Darcy. (1989) "Political Ambition Among Men and Women State Party Leaders." *American Politics Quarterly* 17: 194-207.

Clarke, H., and A. Kornberg. (1979) "Moving Up the Political Escalator: Women Party Officials in the United States and Canada." *Journal of Politics* 41: 1979.

Clucas, R. (1995) "Assessing the First Post-Term Limits Elections in Professional State Legislatures." Presented at the Annual Meeting of the American Political Science Association.

Converse, P. (1964) "The Nature of Belief Systems in Mass Publics." In *Ideology and*

Discontent, D. Apter (ed.). New York: Free Press.

Cook, E. (1987) "Feminism and Group Consciousness in America, 1972 to 1984." Ph.D. dissertation, Ohio State University.

Copeland, G. (1994) "The Closing of Political Minds: Noncandidates in the 4th District of Oklahoma." In *Who Runs for Congress?*, T. Kazee (ed.). Washington, DC: Congressional Quarterly Press.

Costantini, E. (1990) "Political Women and Political Ambition: Closing the Gender Gap." *American Journal of Political Science* 34: 741-770.

Costantini, E., and J.D. Bell. (1984) "Women in Political Parties: Gender Differences in Motives Among California Party Activists." In *Political Women*, J. Flammang (ed.). Beverly Hills, CA: Sage Publications.

Costantini, E., and K. Craik. (1972) "Women as Politicians: The Social Background, Personality, and Political Careers of Female Party Leaders." *Journal of Social Issues* 28: 217-236.

Cotter, C., J. Gibson, J. Bibby, and R. Huckshorn. (1984) *Party Organizations in American Politics*. New York: Praeger.

Currey, V. (1977) "Campaign Theory and Practice--The Gender Variable." In *A Portrait of Marginality: The Political Behavior of American Woman*, M. Githens and J. Prestage (eds.). New York: David McKay Company.

Darcy, R., M. Brewer, and J. Clay. (1984) "Women in the Oklahoma Political System: State Legislative Elections." *Social Science Journal* 21: 67-78.

Darcy, R., and J. Choike. (1986) "A Formal Analysis of Legislative Turnover: Women Candidates and Legislative Representation." *American Journal of Political Science* 30: 237-255.

Darcy, R., and S. Schramm. (1977) "When Women Run Against Men." *Public Opinion Quarterly* 41: 1-12.

Darcy, R., S. Welch, and J. Clark. (1985) "Women Candidates in Single and Multi-Member Districts: American State Legislative Races." *Social Science Quarterly* 66: 945-953.

Darcy, R., S. Welch, and J. Clark. (1994) *Women, Elections, and Representation*. New York: Longman.

Dayhoff, S. (1983) "Sexist Language and Person Perception: Evaluation of Candidates from Newspaper Articles." *Sex Roles* 9: 527-539.

Deaux, K., and L. Lewis. (1984) "The Structure of Gender Stereotypes: The Interrelations Among Components and Gender Label." *Journal of Personality and Social Psychology* 46: 991-1004.

Deber, R. (1982) "The Fault, Dear Brutus: Women as Congressional Candidates in Pennsylvania." *Journal of Politics* 44: 463-479.

Delli Carpini, M., and E. Fuchs. (1993) "The Year of the Woman? Candidates, Voters, and the 1992 Elections." *Political Science Quarterly* 108: 29-36.

Diamond, I. (1977) *Sex Roles in the Statehouse*. New Haven, CT: Yale University Press.

Dilman, D. (1978) *Mail and Telephone Surveys*. New York: John Wiley.

Dipboye, R., H. Fromkin, and K. Wiback. (1975) "Relative Importance of Applicant Sex, Attractiveness, and Scholastic Standing in Evaluation of Job Applicants." *Journal of Applied Psychology* 60: 39-45.

Dubeck, P. (1976) "Women and Access to Political Office: A Comparison of Female and Male State Legislators." *Sociological Quarterly* 17: 42-52.

Duncan, P., and C. Lawrence. (1995) *Politics in America*. Washington, DC: Congressional Quarterly Press.

Dwyre, D., and J. Stonecash. (1992) "Where's the Party? Changing State Party Organizations." *American Politics Quarterly* 20: 326-344.

Eagly, A., M. Makhijani, and B. Klonsky. (1992) "Gender and the Evaluation of Leaders: A

Meta-Analysis." *Psychological Bulletin* 111: 3-32.

Eagly, A., and A. Mladinic. (1989) "Gender Stereotypes and Attitudes Toward Women and Men." *Personality and Social Psychology Bulletin* 15: 543-558.

Eagly, A., and V. Steffen. (1984) "Gender Stereotypes Stem from the Distribution of Women and Men into Social Roles." *Journal of Personality and Social Psychology* 46: 735-753.

Eagly, A., and V. Steffen. (1986) "Gender Stereotypes, Occupational Roles, and Beliefs about Part-Time Employees." *Psychology of Women Quarterly* 10: 252-262.

Eagly, A., and W. Wood. (1982) "Inferred Sex Differences in Status as a Determinant of Gender Stereotypes About Social Influence." *Journal of Personality and Social Psychology* 43: 915-928.

Ekstrand, L., and W. Eckert. (1981) "The Impact of Candidate's Sex on Voter Choice." *Western Political Quarterly* 34: 78-87.

Elazar, D. (1984) *American Federalism: A View from the States*. New York: Crowell.

Eldersveld, S. (1964) *Political Parties*. Chicago: Rand McNally.

Erber, R., and S. Fiske. (1984) "Outcome Dependency and Attention to Inconsistent Information." *Journal of Personality and Social Psychology* 47: 709-726.

Erikson, R. (1978) "Constituency Opinion and Congressional Behavior: A Re-examination of the Miller-Stokes Representational Data." *American Journal of Political Science* 22: 511-535.

Fazio, R., and C. Williams. (1986) "Attitude Accessibility as a Moderator of the Attitude-Perception and Attitude-Behavior Relations: An Investigation of the 1984 Presidential Election." *Journal of Personality and Social Psychology* 51: 505-514.

Ferber, M., J. Huber, and G. Spitze. (1979) "Preference for Men as Bosses and Professionals." *Social Forces* 58: 466-476.

Fiske, S., D. Kinder, and W. M. Larter. (1983) "The Novice and the Expert: Knowledge-Based Strategies in Political Cognition." *Journal of Experimental Social Psychology* 19: 381-400.

Fiske, S., R. Lau, and R. Smith. (1990) "On the Varieties and Utilities of Political Expertise." *Social Cognition* 8: 31-48.

Fiske, S., and S. Taylor. (1991) *Social Cognition*. New York: McGraw-Hill.

Flammang, J. (1984) "Filling the Party Vacuum: Women at the Grassroots Level in Local Politics." In *Political Women*, J. Flammang (ed.). Beverly Hills, CA: Sage Publications.

Fowler, L. (1979) "The Election Lottery: Decisions to Run for Congress." *Public Choice* 34: 399-418.

Fowler, L. (1993) *Candidates, Congress, and the American Democracy*. Ann Arbor: University of Michigan Press.

Fowler, L., and R. McClure. (1989) *Political Ambition*. New Haven, CT: Yale University Press.

Fowlkes, D. (1984a) "Women in Georgia Electoral Politics: 1970-1978." *Social Science Journal* 21: 43-56.

Fowlkes, D. (1984b) "Ambitious Political Women: Counter Socialization and Political Party Context." *Women and Politics* 4: 5-32.

Fowlkes, D., J. Perkins, and S. Rinehart. (1979) "Gender Roles and Party Roles." *American Political Science Review* 73: 772-780.

Frazier, M. (1993) "Factors Influencing the Proportion of Women Nominated and Elected to the Legislatures of Eleven Western Democracies." Master's thesis, Rice University.

Freeman, J. (1986) "The Political Culture of the Democratic and Republican Parties." *Political Science Quarterly* 101: 321-356.

Frendreis, J., J. Gibson, and L. Vertz. (1990) "The Electoral Relevance of Local Party Organizations." *American Political Science Review* 84: 225-235.

Frendreis, J., and A. Gitelson. (1995) "Political Parties, Candidates, and Voters: Winning and

Losing in the 1992 and 1994 State Legislative Elections." Presented at the Annual Meeting of the Southern Political Science Association.

Frendreis, J., A. Gitelson, G. Flemming, and A. Layzell. (1994) "Local Political Parties and Legislative Races in 1992." In *The State of the Parties*, D. Shea and J. Green (eds.). Lanham, MD: Rowman and Littlefield.

Freund, R., and P. Minton. (1979) *Regression Methods*. New York: Marcel Decker.

Funder, D. (1987) "Errors and Mistakes: Evaluating the Accuracy of Social Judgment." *Psychological Bulletin* 101: 75-90.

Gaddie, R., and C. Bullock. (1995) "Congressional Elections and the Year of the Woman: Structural and Elite Influences on Female Candidacies." *Social Science Quarterly* 76: 749-762.

Geiger, S., A. McCulloch, and B. Gergel. (1995) "Motivating Factors and Perceived Behavioral Styles of South Carolina Women Leaders: Comparing the Public, Private, and Nonprofit Sectors." Presented at the Annual Meeting of the Southern Political Science Association.

Gertzog, I. (1979) "Changing Patterns of Female Recruitment to the U.S. House of Representatives." *Legislative Studies Quarterly* 4: 429-445.

Gertzog, I., and M. Simard. (1981) "Women and Hopeless Congressional Candidacies: Nomination Frequency." *American Politics Quarterly* 9: 449-466.

Gibson, J., J. Frendreis, and L. Vertz. (1989) "Party Dynamics in the 1980s: Change in County Party Organizational Strength, 1980-1984." *American Journal of Political Science* 33: 67-90.

Gierzynski, A. (1992) *Legislative Party Campaign Committees in the American States*. Lexington: University Press of Kentucky.

Gierzynski, A., and D. Breaux. (1991) "Money and Votes in State Legislative Elections." *Legislative Studies Quarterly* 16: 203-217.

Giles, M., and A. Evans. (1985) "External Threat, Perceived Threat, and Group Identity." *Social Science Quarterly* 66: 50-65.

Giles, M., and A. Pritchard. (1985) "Campaign Expenditures and Legislative Elections in Florida." *Legislative Studies Quarterly* 10: 71-88.

Gitelson, I., and A. Gitelson. (1981) "Adolescent Attitudes Toward Male and Female Political Candidates." *Women and Politics* 1: 53-64.

Grau, C. (1981) "Competition in State Legislative Primaries." *Legislative Studies Quarterly* 6: 35-54.

Green, J. (1995) "Contextual Factors and Women's Candidacies for Open Seat Elections from 1982-1992." Presented at the Annual Meeting of the American Political Science Association.

Greene, J. (1995) "Term Limits: A Measure of Our Ignorance." *Social Science Quarterly* 76: 717-719.

Gugin L. (1986) "The Impact of Political Structure on the Political Power of Women: A Comparison of Britain and the United States." *Women and Politics* 6: 37-55.

Gurin, P. (1985) "Women's Gender Consciousness." *Public Opinion Quarterly* 49: 143-163.

Hacker, H. (1951) "Women as a Minority Group." *Social Forces* 30: 60-69.

Hain, P. (1974) "Age, Ambitions, and Political Careers: The Middle-Age Crisis." *Western Political Quarterly* 27: 265-274.

Harris, M. (1990) "Effect of Interaction Goals on Expectancy Confirmation in a Problem Solving Context." *Personality and Psychology Bulletin* 16: 521-530.

Harrison, B.C. (1995) "Candidate Gender and Campaign Fund Raising in U.S. House Races." Presented at the Annual Meeting of the American Political Science Association.

Hartman, S., R. Griffeth, L. Miller, and A. Kinicki. (1988) "The Impact of Occupation, Performance, and Sex on Sex Role Stereotyping." *Journal of Social Psychology* 128: 451-463.

Haskell, J., K. Sutten, and P. Squire. (1994) "Old Style Politics and Invisible Challengers: Iowa's 1st and 4th Districts." In *Who Runs for Congress?*, T. Kazee (ed.). Washington, DC: Congressional Quarterly Press.

Hausman, L. (1994) "What's Gender Got to Do With It? Running and Winning at the Local Level." Ph.D. dissertation, Ohio State University.

Hedlund, R., P. Freeman, K. Hamm, and R. Stein. (1979) "The Electability of Women Candidates." *Journal of Politics* 41: 513-524.

Herrick, R. (1995) "A Reappraisal of the Quality of Women Candidates." *Women and Politics* 15: 25-38.

Herrnson, P., and R. Tennant. (1994) "Running for Congress Under the Shadow of the Capitol Dome: The Race for Virginia's 8th District." In *Who Runs for Congress?*, T. Kazee (ed.). Washington, DC: Congressional Quarterly Press.

Hertzke, A. (1994) "Vanishing Candidates in the 2nd District of Colorado." In *Who Runs for Congress?*, T. Kazee (ed.). Washington, DC: Congressional Quarterly Press.

Hill, D. (1981) "Political Culture and Female Represenation." *Journal of Politics* 43: 151-168.

Hoffman, C., and N. Hurst. (1990) "Gender Stereotypes: Perception or Rationalization?" *Journal of Personality and Social Psychology* 58: 197-208.

Hogan, R. (1995) "Campaigning for the State Legislature: Determining Variation in Campaign Organization, Strategy, and Techniques." Presented at the Annual Meeting of the Southern Political Science Association.

Howell, S., and W. Oiler. (1981) "Campaign Activities and Local Election Outcomes." *Social Science Quarterly* 62: 151-160.

Huddy, L., and N. Terkildsen. (1993a) "Gender Stereotypes and the Perception of Male and Female Candidates." *American Journal of Political Science* 37: 119-147.

Huddy, L., and N. Terkildsen. (1993b) "The Consequences of Gender Stereotypes for Women Candidates at Different Levels and Types of Office." *Political Research Quarterly* 46: 503-525.

Hunt, A.L., and R. Pendley. (1972) "Community Gatekeepers: An Examination of Political Recruiters." *Midwest Journal of Political Science* 16: 411-438.

Hyman, H. (1959) *Political Socialization.* Glencoe, IL: Free Press.

Jackman, M., and M. Muha. (1984) "Education and Intergroup Attitudes." *American Sociological Review* 49: 751-769.

Jackson, J., and D. King. (1989) "Public Goods, Private Interests, and Representation." *American Political Science Review* 83: 1143-1164.

Jacob, H. (1962) "Initial Recruitment of Elected Officials in the United States: A Model." *Journal of Politics* 24: 703-716.

Jacobson, G. (1995) "The House Under Term Limits." *Social Science Quarterly* 76: 720-724.

Jennings, M., and B. Farah. (1981) "Social Roles and Political Resources: An Over-Time Study of Men and Women in Party Elites." *American Journal of Political Science* 25: 462-482.

Jennings, M., and N. Thomas. (1968) "Men and Women in Party Elites: Social Roles and Political Resources." *Midwest Journal of Political Science* 12: 469-492.

Jewell, M., and D. Breaux. (1988) "The Effect of Incumbency on State Legislative Elections." *Legislative Studies Quarterly* 13: 495-514.

Jones, E., G. Wood, and G. Quattrone. (1981) "Perceived Variability of Personal Characteristics in In-Groups and Out-Groups." *Personality and Social Psychology Bulletin* 7: 523-528.

Jones, R., and T. Borris. (1985) "Strategic Contributing in Legislative Campaigns: The Case of Minnesota." *Legislative Studies Quarterly* 10: 89-105.

Jones, W., and A. Nelson. (1981) "Correlates of Women's Representation in Lower State Legislative Chambers." *Social Behavior and Personality* 1: 9-15.

Judd, C., and B. Park. (1988) "Out-Group Homogeneity: Judgements of Variability at the Individual and Group Levels." *Journal of Personality and Social Psychology* 54: 778-788.

Jussim, L. (1990) "Social Reality and Social Problems: The Role of Expectancies." *Journal of Social Issues* 46: 9-34.

Jussim, L., and J. Eccles. (1992) "Teacher Expectations: Construction and Reflection of Student Achievement." *Journal of Personality and Social Psychology* 63: 947-961.

Kahn, K. (1992) "Does Being Male Help?" *Journal of Politics* 54: 497-517.

Kahn, K., and E. Goldenberg. (1991) "Women Candidates in the News: An Examination of Gender Differences in U.S. Senate Campaign Coverage." *Public Opinion Quarterly* 55: 180-199.

Kahn, W., and F. Crosby. (1987) "Discriminating Between Attitudes and Discriminatory Behaviors." In *Women and Work: An Annual Review*, L. Larwood, B. Gutek, and A. Stromberg (eds.). Beverly Hills, CA: Sage Publications.

Kaid, L., S. Myers, V. Pipps, and J. Hunter. (1984) "Sex Role Perceptions and Televised Political Advertising." *Women and Politics* 4: 41-54.

Karnig, A., and O. Walter. (1976) "Election of Women to City Councils." *Social Science Quarterly* 56: 605-613.

Kathlene, L. (1989) "Uncovering the Political Impacts of Gender: An Exploratory Study." *Western Political Quarterly* 42: 397-421.

Kathlene, L. (1994) "Power and Influence in State Legislative Policymaking: The Interaction of Gender and Position in Committee Hearing Debates." *American Political Science Review* 88: 560-576.

Kathlene, L. (1995) "Alternative Views of Crime: Legislative Policymaking in Gendered Terms." *Journal of Politics* 57: 696-723.

Kayden, X., and E. Mahe. (1985) *The Party Goes On: The Persistence of the Two-Party System in the United States.* New York: Basic Books.

Kazee, T. (1994a) "The Emergence of Congressional Candidates." In *Who Runs for Congress?*, T. Kazee (ed.). Washington, DC: Congressional Quarterly Press.

Kazee, T. (1994b) "Ambition and Candidacy: Running as a Strategic Calculation." In *Who Runs for Congress?*, T. Kazee (ed.). Washington, DC: Congressional Quarterly Press.

Kazee, T., and S. Roberts. (1994) "Challenging a 'Safe' Incumbent: Latent Competition in North Carolina's 9th District." In *Who Runs for Congress?*, T. Kazee (ed.). Washington, DC: Congressional Quarterly Press.

Kazee, T., and M. Thornberry. (1990) "Where's the Party? Congressional Candidate Recruitment and American Party Organizations." *Western Political Quarterly* 43: 61-80.

Kiesler, S.B. (1975) "Actuarial Prejudice Toward Women and Its Implications." *Journal of Applied Social Psychology* 5: 201-216.

Kingdon, J. (1966) *Candidates for Office: Beliefs and Strategies.* New York: Random House.

Kirkpatrick, J. (1974) *Political Woman.* New York: Basic Books.

Kirkpatrick, J. (1978) *Dismantling the Parties: Reflections on Party Reform and Party Decomposition.* Washington, DC: American Enterprise Institute.

Klahr, D. (1969) "Decision Making in a Complex Environment: The Use of Similarity Judgements to Predict Preferences." *Management Science* 15: 593-618.

Ladd, E.C., and C. Hadley. (1975) *Transformations of the American Party System: Political Coalitions from the New Deal to the 1970s.* New York: W.W. Norton.

Lamson, P. (1968) *Few Are Chosen: American Women in Political Life Today.* Boston: Houghton Mifflin Company.

Lane, R. (1959) *Political Life: Why People Get Involved in Politics.* Glencoe, IL: Free Press.

Larrow, M., and M. Wiener. (1992) "Stereotypes and Desirability Ratings for Female and Male Roles." In *New Directions in Feminist Psychology*, J. Chrisler and D. Howard (eds.). New York: Springer Publishing Company.

Lau, R. (1995) "Information Search During an Election Campaign: Introducing a Processing-Tracing Methodology for Political Scientists." In *Political Judgment: Structure and Process*, M. Lodge and K. McGraw (eds.). Ann Arbor: University of Michigan Press.

Lau, R., and D. Russell. (1980) "Attributions in the Sports Pages." *Journal of Personality and Social Psychology* 39: 29-38.

Lawson, K. (1980) "California: The Uncertainties of Reform." In *Party Renewal in America*, G. Pomper (ed.). New York: Praeger.

Layzell, A., and L.M. Overby. (1994) "Biding Their Time in the Illinios 9th." In *Who Runs for Congress?*, T. Kazee (ed.). Washington, DC: Congressional Quarterly Press.

Lee, M. (1976) "Why Few Women Hold Public Office: Democracy and Sexual Roles." *Political Science Quarterly* 91: 297-314.

Lee, M. (1977) "Toward Understanding Why Few Women Hold Public Office: Factors Affecting the Participation of Women in Local Politics." In *A Portrait of Marginality: The Political Behavior of American Woman*, M. Githens and J. Prestage (eds.). New York: David McKay Company.

Leeper, M. (1991) "The Impact of Prejudice on Female Candidates: An Experimental Look at Voter Inference." *American Politics Quarterly* 19: 248-261.

Leeper, M. (1996) "Springboard or Vacuum? Women, State Legislatures, and Political Ambition." Presented at the Annual Meeting of the Southern Political Science Association.

Leowenberg, G., and S. Patterson. (1979) *Comparative Legislatures.* Boston: Little, Brown, and Company.

Lilley, W., L. DeFranco, and W. Diefenderer. (1994) *The Almanac of State Legislatures.* Washington, DC: Congressional Quarterly Press.

Linville, P., and E. Jones. (1980) "Polarized Appraisals of Out-Group Members." *Journal of Personality and Social Psychology* 38: 689-703.

Lorenzi-Cioldi, F. (1993) "They All Look Alike, But So Do We . . . Sometimes: Perceptions of In-Group and Out-Group Homogeneity as a Function of Sex and Contact." *British Journal of Social Psychology* 32: 111-124.

Luttrell, W. (1988) "The Edison School Struggle: The Reshaping of Working-Class Education and Women's Consciousness." In *Women and the Politics of Empowerment*, A. Bookman and S. Morgen (eds.). Philadelphia: Temple University Press.

Mackie, D., and L. Worth. (1989) "Differential Recall of Subcategory Information about In-Group and Out-Group Members." *Personality and Social Psychology Bulletin* 15: 401-413.

MacManus, S. (1981) "A City's First Female Officeholder: Coattails for Future Female Officeholders." *Western Political Quarterly* 34: 88-89.

Main, E., G. Gryski, and B. Shapiro. (1984) "Different Perspectives: Southern State Legislators' Attitudes About Women in Politics." *Social Science Journal* 21: 21-28.

Maisel, L.S. (1981) "Congressional Elections in 1978: The Road to Nomination, the Road to Election." *American Politics Quarterly* 9: 23-47.

Mandel, R. (1981) *In the Running: the New Woman Candidate.* Boston: Beacon Press.

Mandel, R., and D. Dodson. (1992) "Do Women Officeholders Make a Difference?" In *The American Woman*, S. Rix (ed.). New York: W.W. Norton.

Margolis, D. (1980) "The Invisible Hands: Sex Roles and the Division of Labor in Two Local Political Parties." In *Women in Local Politics*, D. Stewart (ed.). Metuchen, NJ: Scarecrow Press.

Marietti, M. (1992) "Boards Which Hire Female Superintendents: Profiles, Comparisons, and Contextual Perspectives." Ed.D. dissertation, Arizona State University.

Marvick, D. (1980) "Party Organizational Personnel and Electoral Democracy in Los Angeles, 1963-1972." In *The Party Symbol: Readings on Political Parties*, W. Crotty (ed.). San Francisco: Freeman.

Matland, R., and D. Brown. (1992) "District Magnitude's Effect on Female Representation in U.S. State Legislatures." *Legislative Studies Quarterly* 17: 469-492.

Matthews, D. (1984) "Legislative Recruitment and Legislative Careers." *Legislative Studies Quarterly* 9: 547-586.

Mattison, G., and S. Storey. (1992) *Women in Citizen Advocacy*. Jefferson, NC: McFarland and Company.

McDonald, J., and V.H. Pierson. (1984) "Female County Party Leaders and the Perception of Discrimination: A Test of the Male Conspiracy Theory." *Social Science Journal* 21: 13-20.

McGraw, K., and N. Pinney. (1990) "The Effects of General and Domain-Specific Expertise on Political Memory and Judgment." *Social Cognition* 8: 9-30.

McLean, J. (1994) "Strategic Choices: Career Decisions of Elected Women." Ph.D. dissertation, Ohio State University.

McWilliams, W.C. (1980) "Parties as Civic Associations." In *Party Renewal in America*, G. Pomper (ed.). New York: Praeger.

Merritt, S. (1980) "Sex Differences in Role Behavior and Policy Orientations of Suburban Officeholders." In *Women in Local Politics*, D. Stewart (ed.). Metuchen, NJ: Scarecrow Press.

Messe, L., and B. Watts. (1980) "Self-pay Behavior: Sex Differences in Reliance on External Cues and Feelings of Comfort." *Academic Psychology Bulletin* 2: 83-88.

Mezey, S. (1978a) "Does Sex Make a Difference? A Case Study of Women in Politics." *Western Political Quarterly* 31: 492-501.

Mezey, S. (1978b) "Women and Representation: The Case of Hawaii." *Journal of Politics* 40: 369-385.

Mezey, S. (1980) "Perceptions of Women's Roles on Local Councils in Connecticut." In *Women in Local Politics*, D. Stewart (ed.). Metuchen, NJ: Scarecrow Press.

Mezey, S. (1994) "Increasing the Number of Women in Office: Does It Matter?" In *The Year of the Woman: Myths and Realities*, E. Cook, S. Thomas, and C. Wilcox (eds.). Boulder, CO: Westview Press.

Michels, R. (1962) [1915] *Political Parties: A Sociological Study of the Oligarchial Tendencies of Modern Democracy*. New York: Crowell-Collier Books.

Miller, L. (1986) "Political Recruitment and Electoral Success: A Look at Sex Differences in Municipal Elections." *Social Science Journal* 23: 75-90.

Millett, K. (1971) *Sexual Politics*. New York: Avon.

Moncrief, G. (1992) "The Increase in Campaign Expenditures in State Legislative Elections." *Western Political Quarterly* 44: 549-558.

Moncrief, G., and J. Thompson. (1995) "State Legislative Campaign Financing in the 1994 Election: The Cases of the North Carolina and Washington Houses." Presented at the Annual Meeting of the Southern Political Science Association.

Moncrief, G., and J. Thompson. (1992) "Electoral Structure and State Legislative Representation." *Journal of Politics* 54: 246-256.

Montjoy, R., W. Shaffer, and R. Weber. (1980) "Policy Preferences of Party Elites and Masses: Conflict or Consensus?" *American Politics Quarterly* 8: 319-343.

Morgen, S. (1988) "'It's the Whole Power of the City Against Us!' The Development of Political Consciousness in a Women's Health Care Coalition." In *Women and the Politics of Empowerment*, A. Bookman and S. Morgen (eds.). Philadelphia: Temple University Press.

Moscow, W. (1948) *Politics in the Empire State*. New York: Knopf.

Nechemias, C. (1985) "Geographic Mobility and Women's Access to State Legislatures." *Western Political Quarterly* 38: 119-131.

Nechemias, C. (1987) "Changes in the Election of Women to U.S. State Legislative Seats." *Legislative Studies Quarterly* 12: 125-142.

Niemi, R., and L. Winsky. (1987) "Membership Turnover in U.S. State Legislatures: Trends and Effects of Districting." *Legislative Studies Quarterly* 12: 115-123.

Niven, D. (1997) "State Party Committees and Women's Legislative Candidacies: Recruitment as Help or Hindrance?" Presented at the Annual Meeting of the Midwest Political Science Association.

Norris, P., and J. Lovenduski. (1993) "If Only More Candidates Came Forward: Supply-Side Explanations of Candidate Selection in Britain." *British Journal of Political Science* 23: 373-408.

Oppenheimer, B. (1995) "House Term Limits: A Distorted Picture." *Social Science Quarterly* 76: 725-729.

Orum, A., R. Cohen, S. Grasmuck, and A. Orum. (1977) "Sex, Socialization, and Politics." In *A Portrait of Marginality: The Political Behavior of American Women*, M. Githens and J. Prestage (eds.). New York: David McKay Company.

Palisi, B., and C. Canning. (1991) "Perceived Control Among Well Educated Men and Women." *Humboldt Journal of Social Relations* 16: 93-110.

Paolino, P. (1995) "Group-Salient Issues and Group Representation: Support for Women Candidates in the 1992 Senate Elections." *American Journal of Political Science* 39: 294-313.

Patterson, S., and G. Boynton. (1970) "Legislative Recruitment in a Civic Culture." *Social Science Quarterly* 50: 243-262.

Perkins, J., and D. Fowlkes. (1980) "Opinion Representation versus Social Representation, or Why Women Can't Run as Women and Win." *American Political Science Review* 74: 92-103.

Piliavin, J. (1987) "Age, Race, and Sex Similarity to Candidates and Voting Preference." *Journal of Applied Social Psychology* 17: 351-368.

Pomper, G. (1965) "New Jersey County Chairmen." *Western Political Quarterly* 18: 186-197.

Pomper, G. (1992) *Passions and Interests: Political Party Concepts of American Democracy.* Lawrence: University of Kansas Press.

Prewitt, K. (1970) *The Recruitment of Political Leaders*. Indianapolis: The Bobbs-Merrill Company.

Pritchard, A. (1992) "Changes in Electoral Structures and the Success of Women Candidates: The Case of Florida." *Social Science Quarterly* 73: 62-70.

Procter, D., W. Schenck-Hamlin, and K. Haase. (1994) "Exploring the Role of Gender in the Development of Negative Political Advertisements." *Women and Politics* 14: 1-22.

Rapoport, R., K. Metcalf, and J. Hartman. (1989) "Candidate Traits and Voter Inferences: An Experimental Study." *Journal of Politics* 51: 917-932.

Rasmussen, J. (1983) "The Electoral Costs of Being a Woman in the 1979 British General Election." *Comparative Politics* 15: 461-475.

Reed, W.R., and D.E. Schansberg. (1995) "The House Under Term Limits: What Would It

Look Like?" *Social Science Quarterly* 76: 699-716.

Reeves, T. (1991) *A Question of Character.* New York: Free Press.

Reingold, B. (1992) "Concepts of Representation Among Female and Male State Legislators." *Legislative Studies Quarterly* 17: 509-537.

Richardson, L., and P. Freeman. (1995) "Gender Differences in Constituency Service Among State Legislators." *Political Research Quarterly* 48: 169-179

Rosenberg, S., L. Bohan, P. McCafferty, and K. Harris. (1986) "The Image and the Vote: The Effect of Candidate Presentation on Voter Preference." *American Journal of Political Science* 30: 108-127.

Rosenstone, S., and J.M. Hansen. (1993) *Mobilization, Participation, and Democracy in America.* New York: Macmillan Publishing Company.

Rosenthal, A. (1974) "Turnover in State Legislatures." *American Journal of Political Science* 18: 609-616.

Rosenthal, C. (1996) "A View of Their Own: Women's Committee Experiences as a Lens on State Legislatures." Presented at the Annual Meeting of the Midwest Political Science Association.

Rosenwasser, S., and N. Dean. (1989) "Gender Role and Political Office." *Psychology of Women Quarterly* 13: 77-85.

Rosenwasser, S., R. Rogers, S. Fling, K. Silvers-Pickens, and J. Butemeyer. (1987) "Attitudes Toward Women and Men in Politics: Perceived Male and Female Candidate Competencies and Participant Personality Characteristics." *Political Psychology* 8: 191-200.

Rossi, A. (1983) "Beyond the Gender Gap: Women's Bid for Political Power." *Social Science Quarterly* 64: 718-733.

Rozsnafszky, J., and D. Hendel. (1977) "Relationship Between Ego Development and Attitudes Toward Women." *Psychological Reports* 41: 161-162.

Rule, W. (1981) "Why Women Don't Run: The Critical Contextual Factors in Women's Legislative Recruitment." *Western Political Quarterly* 34: 60-77.

Rule, W. (1987) "Electoral Systems, Contextual Factors and Women's Opportunity for Election to Parliament in 23 Democracies." *Western Political Quarterly* 40: 477-498.

Rule, W. (1990) "Why More Women Are State Legislators." *Western Political Quarterly* 43: 437-448.

Sacks, K. (1988) "Gender and Grassroots Leadership." In *Women and the Politics of Empowerment*, A. Bookman and S. Morgen (eds.). Philadelphia: Temple University Press.

Saint-Germain, M. (1989) "Does Their Difference Make a Difference? The Impact of Women on Public Policy in the Arizona Legislature." *Social Science Quarterly* 70: 956-968.

Sapiro, V. (1981a) "When Are Interests Interesting? The Problem of Political Representation of Women." *American Political Science Review* 75: 701-716.

Sapiro, V. (1981b) "If Senator Baker Were a Woman: An Experimental Study of Candidate Images." *Political Psychology* 2: 61-83.

Sapiro, V. (1982) "Private Costs of Public Commitments or Public Costs of Private Commitments? Family Roles versus Political Ambition." *American Journal of Political Science* 26: 265-279.

Sapiro, V., and B. Farah. (1980) "New Pride and Old Prejudice: Political Ambition and Role Orientations Among Female Partisan Elites." *Women and Politics* 1: 13-36.

Schlenker, B., and R. Miller. (1977) "Egocentrism in Groups: Self-Serving Biases or Logical Information Processing?" *Journal of Personality and Social Psychology* 35: 755-764.

Schlozman, K., N. Burns, and S. Verba. (1994) "Gender and the Pathways to Participation: The Role of Resources." *Journal of Politics* 56: 963-990.

Schramm, S. (1981) "Women and Representation: Self Government and Role Change." *Western Political Quarterly* 34: 46-59.

Seligman, L. (1961) "Political Recruitment and Party Structure: A Case Study." *American Political Science Review* 60: 77-86.

Seligman, L., M. King, C.L. Kim, and R. Smith. (1974) *Patterns of Recruitment*. Chicago: Rand McNally.

Shea, D. (1995) *Transforming Democracy: Legislative Campaign Committees and Political Parties*. Albany: State University of New York Press.

Sheffield, J., and L. Goering. (1978) "Winning and Losing: Candidate Advantage in Local Elections." *American Politics Quarterly* 6: 453-468.

Shin, K., and J. Jackson. (1979) "Membership Turnover in U.S. State Legislatures: 1931-1976." *Legislative Studies Quarterly* 4: 95-104.

Shingles, R. (1981) "Black Consciousness and Political Participation: The Missing Link." *American Political Science Review* 75: 76-90.

Sigelman, C., D. Thomas, L. Sigelman, and F. Ribich. (1986) "Gender, Physical Attractiveness, and Electability: An Experimental Investigation of Voter Biases." *Journal of Applied Social Psychology* 16: 229-248.

Sigelman, L., C. Sigelman, and C. Fowler. (1987) "A Bird of a Different Feather? An Experimental Investigation of Physical Attractiveness and the Electability of Female Candidates." *Social Psychology Quarterly* 50: 32-43.

Sigelman, L., and S. Welch (1984) "Race, Gender, and Opinion Toward Black and Female Presidential Candidates." *Public Opinion Quarterly* 48: 467-475.

Simon, R., and J. Landis. (1989) "Women's and Men's Attitudes about a Woman's Place and Role." *Public Opinion Quarterly* 53: 265-276.

Smith, K. (1976) "The Characteristics and Motivations of American Women Who Seek Positions of Political Leadership." Ph.D. dissertation, New School for Social Research.

Sniderman, P., T. Piazza, P. Tetlock, and A. Kendrick. (1991) "The New Racism." *American Journal of Political Science* 35: 423-447.

Snyder, M. (1984) "When Belief Creates Reality." In *Advances in Experimental Social Psychology*, L. Berkowitz (ed.). San Diego: Academic Press.

Snyder, M., and P. Miene. (1994) "Stereotyping of the Elderly: A Functional Approach." *British Journal of Social Psychology* 33: 63-82.

Soule, J., and W. McGrath. (1977) "A Comparative Study of Male-Female Political Attitudes at Citizen and Elite Levels." In *A Portrait of Marginality: The Political Behavior of American Woman*, M. Githens and J. Prestage (eds.). New York: David McKay Company.

Spence, J.T., R. Helmreich, and J. Stapp. (1975) "Ratings of Self and Peers on Sex Role Attributes and Their Relation to Self-Esteem and Conceptions of Masculinity and Femininity." *Journal of Personality and Social Psychology* 32: 29-39.

Steinbeck, J. (1945) *Cannery Row*. New York: Penguin Books.

Stivers, C. (1993) *Gender Images in Public Administration*. Newbury Park, CA: Sage Publications.

Stonecash, J. (1988) "Working at the Margins: Campaign Finance and Party Strategy in New York Assembly Elections." *Legislative Studies Quarterly* 13: 477-493.

Studlar, D., and I. McAllister. (1991) "Political Recruitment to the Australian Legislature: Toward an Explanation of Women's Electoral Disadvantages." *Western Political Quarterly* 44: 467-485.

Studlar, D., and S. Welch. (1987) "Understanding the Iron Law of Andrarchy: The Effects of Candidate Gender on Voting for Local Office in Scotland." *Comparative Political Studies* 20: 174-191.

Studlar, D., and S. Welch. (1991) "Does District Magnitude Matter? Women Candidates in London Local Elections." *Western Political Quarterly* 44: 457-466.

Tedin, K., D. Brady, and A. Vedlitz. (1977) "Sex Differences in Political Attitudes and

Behavior." *Journal of Politics* 39: 448-456.

Tetlock, P. (1983) "Accountability and Complexity of Thought." *Journal of Personality and Social Psychology* 45: 74-83.

Thomas, S. (1994) *How Women Legislate*. New York: Oxford University Press.

Thompson, J., W. Cassie, and M. Jewell. (1994) "A Sacred Cow or Just a Lot of Bull? Party and PAC Money in State Legislative Elections." *Political Research Quarterly* 47: 223-237.

Thompson, J., and G. Moncrief. (1993) "The Implications of Term Limits for Women and Minorities." *Social Science Quarterly* 74: 300-309.

Thornton, A., D. Alwin, and D. Camburn. (1983) "Causes and Consequences of Sex-Role Attitudes and Attitude Change." *American Sociological Review* 48: 211-227.

Tucker, H. (1986) "Contextual Models of Participation in U.S. State Legislative Elections." *Western Political Quarterly* 39: 67-78.

Tucker, H., and R. Weber. (1987) "State Legislative Election Outcomes: Contextual Effects and Legislative Performance Effects." *Legislative Studies Quarterly* 12: 537-553.

Turner, J., R. Brown, and H. Tajfel. (1979) "Social Comparison and Group Interest in Ingroup Favoritism." *European Journal of Social Psychology* 9: 187-204.

Uhlaner, C., and K. Schlozman. (1986) "Candidate Gender and Congressional Campaign Receipts." *Journal of Politics* 48: 30-50.

Upshaw, E. (1995) "An Economist's View of Research on Term Limits." *Social Science Quarterly* 76: 734-740.

Van Hightower, N. (1977) "The Recruitment of Women in Public Office." *American Politics Quarterly* 5: 301-314.

Van Horn, C. (1993) "The Quiet Revolution." In *The State of the States*, C. Van Horn (ed.). Washington, DC: Congressional Quarterly Press.

Vandenbosch, S. (1995) "Evidence for an Inverse Relationship Between the Percentage of Women State Legislators and the Percentage of Christian Church Adherents in the States." Presented at the Annual Meeting of the Southern Political Science Association.

Volgy, T., E. Schwartz, and H. Gottlieb. (1986) "Female Representation and the Quest for Resources: Feminist Activism and Electoral Success." *Social Science Quarterly* 66: 156-168.

Welch, S. (1977) "Women as Political Animals? A Test of Some Explanations for Male-Female Political Participation Differences." *American Journal of Political Science* 4: 711-730.

Welch, S. (1978) "Recruitment of Women to Public Office." *Western Political Quarterly* 31: 372-380.

Welch, S., M. Ambrosius, J. Clark, and R. Darcy. (1984) "The Effect of Candidate Gender on Electoral Outcome in State Legislative Races." *Western Political Quarterly* 38: 464-475.

Welch, S., and A. Karnig. (1979) "Correlates of Female Office Holding." *Journal of Politics* 41: 478-491.

Welch, S., and L. Sigelman. (1982) "Changes in Public Attitudes Toward Women in Politics." *Social Science Quarterly* 63: 312-321.

Welch, S., and D. Studlar. (1988) "The Effects of Candidate Gender on Voting for Local Office in England." *British Journal of Political Science* 18: 273-281.

Welch, S., and D. Studlar. (1990) "Multi Member Districts and the Representation of Women: Evidence from Britain and the U.S." *Journal of Politics* 52: 391-412.

Welch, W. (1976) "Effectiveness of Expenditures in State Legislative Races." *American Politics Quarterly* 4: 333-355.

Werner, B. (1993) "Bias in the Electoral Process: Mass and Elite Attitudes and Female State Legislative Candidates; 1982-1990." Ph.D. dissertation, Washington University.

Werner, E. (1968) "Women in State Legislatures." *Western Political Quarterly* 21: 40-50.

Werner, P., and G.W. LaRussa. (1985) "Persistence and Change in Sex Role Stereotypes." *Sex Roles* 12: 1089-1100.

White, T. (1961) *The Making of the President 1960*. New York: Atheneum Publishers.

Wilcox, C. (1994) "Why Was 1992 the 'Year of the Woman'? Explaining Women's Gains in 1992." In *The Year of the Woman: Myths and Realities*, E. Cook, S. Thomas, and C. Wilcox (eds.). Boulder, CO: Westview Press.

Wilhite, A., and J. Theilman. (1987) "Women, Blacks, and PAC Discrimination." *Social Science Quarterly* 67: 283-298.

Winter, D., A. Stewart, and D. McClelland. (1977) "Husband's Motives and Wife's Career Level." *Journal of Personality and Social Psychology* 35: 159-166.

Yoder, J. (1994) "Looking Beyond Numbers: The Effects of Gender Status, Job Prestige, and Occupational Gender-Typing on Tokenism Processes." *Social Psychology Quarterly* 57: 150-159.

Yount, K. (1986) "A Theory of Productive Activity: The Relationships Among Self-Concept, Gender, Sex Role Stereotypes, and Work-Emergent Traits." *Psychology of Women Quarterly* 10: 63-88.

Zepatos, T., and E. Kaufman. (1995) *Women for a Change: A Grassroots Guide to Activism and Politics*. New York: Facts on File.

Zilber, J. (1996) "Political Movements, Group Consciousness, and Participation in America." Ph.D. dissertation, Ohio State University.

Zipp, J., and E. Plutzer. (1985) "Gender Differences in Voting for Female Candidates: Evidence from the 1982 Election." *Public Opinion Quarterly* 49: 179-197.

Index

About the Author

DAVID NIVEN is Assistant Professor of Political Science at Florida Atlantic University.

ISBN 0-275-96073-0

90000>

EAN

9 780275 960735

HARDCOVER BAR CODE